Writing a Postgraduate Thesis or Dissertation

Tools for Success

Michael Hammond

Routledge
Taylor & Francis Group

LONDON AND NEW YORK

Cover image: © Getty Images

First published 2023
by Routledge
4 Park Square, Milton Park, Abingdon, Oxon OX14 4RN

and by Routledge
605 Third Avenue, New York, NY 10158

*Routledge is an imprint of the Taylor & Francis Group,
an informa business*

© 2023 Michael Hammond

British Library Cataloguing-in-Publication Data
A catalogue record for this book is available from the British Library

Library of Congress Cataloging-in-Publication Data
A catalog record has been requested for this book

ISBN: 9780367752811 (hbk)
ISBN: 9780367752828 (pbk)
ISBN: 9781003161820 (ebk)

DOI: 10.4324/9781003161820

Typeset in Warnock Pro
by KnowledgeWorks Global Ltd.

Writing a Postgraduate Thesis or Dissertation

Writing a Postgraduate Thesis or Dissertation discusses the challenges that students encounter in their writing and provides thoughtful advice on how to address those challenges. It provides guidance on writing about literature, methodology and methods and shows the importance of stating a contribution to knowledge.

Providing key insight into the process of writing a dissertation or thesis, this book

- explains the process of writing and provides insight into strategies that support good writing
- considers the audience and purpose of a report as well as the voice of the writer
- discusses the structure and organisational features of theses and dissertations, highlighting the central role of the research question

Writing a Postgraduate Thesis or Dissertation is an ideal guide for doctoral and masters students in the social sciences.

Michael Hammond is a Reader in the Centre for Education Studies at the University of Warwick, UK.

Routledge Study Skills

Writing a Postgraduate Thesis or Dissertation
Tools for Success
Michael Hammond

Studying Online
Succeeding through Distance Learning at University
Graham Jones

For more information about this series, please visit: https://www.routledge.com/Routledge-Study-Skills/book-series/ROUTLEDGESS

Contents

List of figures and tables

Preface

The aim of this book is to help you in reporting a research project you have carried out, in particular to assist you in writing a dissertation or thesis. It does this by showing how you can write about your field of research, about the tradition of methodology and methods in which you are working, and about the contribution to knowledge you are making. Writing a dissertation or thesis is not easy, not least because there are different views on what counts as appropriate methodology, what makes a contribution and, for that matter, what is knowledge in the first place. This leaves you with a challenge. However, you can meet this challenge if you keep the expectations of your reader in the front of your mind.

There are a great many books on writing at higher degree level, so why another one? The contribution of this book is to present a holistic picture of writing social research. First, you need knowledge of writing as a process and an awareness of the strategies that help you become a productive writer. Second, you need knowledge of the way that academic reports are organised and the different tones that academics strike when writing about their studies. Third, you need knowledge of research methods, including an appreciation of the central role of the research questions and the nature of social research. This book will help show how you can develop strategies to enable you to draw on these different kinds of knowledge when you write.

▶ Guide to the book

The book is divided into six chapters. The first deals with writing in general. It celebrates writing as a way of allowing communication across time and distance while recognising the mental challenge of writing and the need for support and feedback. There are routines and strategies you can use to help address blocks on writing and ways to ease the process. For example, writing can be broken down into stages, something we illustrate with an example of writing about community of practice. We then make the point that all texts are written with audiences in mind and readers, particularly the examiners who are reading your thesis or dissertation, want to see three things: Your knowledge of a field; the application of a methodology; a contribution to knowledge. The following chapters deal with each of these in turn.

Chapter 2 looks at ways of showing knowledge of a field of research. We begin by discussing reading and go on to look at ways of accessing literature, strategies for active reading, and the taking of notes. We discuss how to turn notes into coherent reporting and explain the importance of 'frames' for writing – these can be tables or simply headers which help you organise what you want to write. We look, too, at conceptual and theoretical frameworks and how these may form an important part of some, but not all, reports. We stress that there are different stances to take on the literature. Some researchers are deferential, seeing the literature as providing a secure knowledge base on which their own research can tentatively build. Others have a more 'profane' stance; they are more focused on the gaps and the biases. Both stances have strengths and limitations and part of being critical is to weigh up the value of each and to present a stance of your own.

In Chapter 3, we look at methodologies and methods. All research projects begin with a question even if, for some researchers, questions are very open-ended and change during the project. Questions are the thread that holds a project together and there should be a close relationship between questions, methodology and method. Discussion of methodology needs to consider the nature of social research, but should also set out the 'nuts and bolts' of your data collection and how your data were analysed. Again, a critical stance is needed. A thesis or dissertation needs to describe the strengths of the research but recognise that other approaches and other interpretations are possible.

Chapter 4 takes us into writing about a contribution to knowledge. Here, you need to be confident when setting out your findings while recognising limitations and things that could have been done differently. A key point is that the reader is interested in the detail of a particular project but also wants to understand what is transferable or relatable from this study to other contexts. Most researchers will want to write not just about their contribution to theoretical knowledge but also to make practical recommendations for the different stakeholders involved in the projects.

After having looked at the content of a report in the previous three chapters, we now move in Chapter 5 to the organisation of a research report. We discuss the hold the 'standard' format (introduction/ literature review/methodology/findings/discussion) has as a frame for writing a dissertation or thesis. We describe the strengths of this format but the reasons why alternatives are sometimes used. We look at the role of signposting and sequencing in all report writing as well as the importance of using academic vocabulary and of expressing yourself clearly and accessibly. We discuss how you can develop a voice in your writing, using examples from the literature. The importance of proofreading is covered, no matter how irksome you may find this when it comes to your own writing.

A final shorter chapter reprises the important themes within the book and provides a reminder of the different kinds of knowledge and know-how you need to draw on in writing your report. A dissertation or thesis should take the reader on a journey from identifying a problem, devising strategies to address that problem, and setting out what we know now in the light of the study. You do not need to have a special talent for writing to write a valuable research report just make your meaning clear, be assertive about what you have achieved, but also critical and measured.

Each chapter contains examples of writing from different research contexts. Some of these are excerpts from articles in journals or books, but most are short vignettes in the style of a thesis or dissertation. These vignettes are taken from a range of contexts, including community of practice, online courses, riots and why some people riot, tourism and holiday destinations. Go to the 'where to read more' sections at the end of each chapter if these topics particularly interest you. However, no special knowledge of any of the contexts is expected.

I hope the book gives you, the reader, encouragement to write, strategies for writing, and the motivation to add your voice to the academic community. The book has emerged out of several years of supervising students, often international students, at masters, and doctorate level. I would like to thank these students for opening up on their writing strategies, as well as colleagues who have helped me develop my own writing over time. Finally, I would like to thank Penny Nunn for having the patience to read several versions of the text. Anything I have got wrong is my own responsibility.

About writing

We begin by looking at the nature of writing and at ideas for helping us to become more effective writers. This chapter is divided into the following sections:

- Why is writing important?
- Why is writing a challenge?
- How can you become a more productive writer?
- Thinking about the process of writing
- An example of planning and writing

▶ WHY IS WRITING IMPORTANT?

Writing is important as it is the way we communicate across time and distance. We can reflect on our origins as a species from Darwin; we can use Plato's dialogues to investigate the nature of truth; we can use Confucius to explore concepts of sincerity; and we can articulate the rights of the citizen from Thomas Paine and from Mary Wollstonecraft the rights of women. In the world of social research, we can learn of the importance of social class from reading Marx; from Durkheim, we can follow the first coherent attempts at causal explanations for social phenomena;

DOI: 10.4324/9781003161820-1

and from Weber, we can appreciate the importance of beliefs in shaping economic systems. We can read contemporary accounts of topics including the influence of social pressure on decision making; how and why people riot; why populism appeals to some people but not to others; the influence of social networks on childhood; and on so much else besides. It is all there for us to praise, criticise, and reinterpret as we have access to texts. Texts allow us to both build on the past and, just as important, to know when we want to make a complete break and think about society in a new way. Of course, in modern times, speeches and films as well as written texts can be recorded and these provide important sources of information too, but written text provides the most efficient way we have to pass ideas from one context to another.

Writing is not only about communicating to others, it is about communicating to ourselves. No one fully understands how language works but we have all experienced that shift from half-formed association in our mind to tangible statement on the page. Language enables us to get our stories straight and writing plays a particularly important role as it allows us to refine what we want to express even as we write it. Writing lets us to find out more about who we are and to present a version of ourselves to the communities to which we belong. One very important function of writing is that it enables us to discover what we did not know we knew.

Writing is particularly helpful as we can only hold so much in our short-term memory. For example, if we try to remember four new items, say four new words in a foreign language, we will probably have forgotten them by the end of the day – and if we had held on to them, we would have expended a lot of mental energy in doing so. Put the same words on paper, or on screen, and we can retrieve them whenever we need to. Writing allows us to 'park' facts and ideas so we can get on with other thinking until we are ready to go back. Writing is a tool for remembering.

Writing is core to the experience of study as education is about both the communication of ideas and about self-discovery and learning to learn. Academic writing is not so much about recalling or describing events but offering an interpretation of events – *the reasons for* the Arab Spring, *the role of* social cohesion through charitable giving, and *the rationale* for school reform. Academics employ a quite abstract and specialised vocabulary to express themselves. They talk about concepts that are *explored*, perspectives which are *expanded upon*, data which is *mined*, and shortcomings which are *identified*. Not surprisingly, much academic assessment requires students to write discursive texts and teachers typically spend a lot of time assessing those texts and providing students with extensive feedback on their writing. For sure, there is innovation in the process of assessment. Students may be expected to talk about their ideas, and in some cases, the viva is central to assessment at both masters and doctoral levels. Students will often take part in assessed group presentations, and even in joint performance, and some may produce multimedia content. All this is fine, variety is to be welcomed. However, students are nearly always expected at some point to write an extended reflective report and you will not get far in academia without producing a thesis or dissertation or both.

▶ WHY IS WRITING A CHALLENGE?

Writing is important in academia and for some it is pleasurable, even a joy, but it is also difficult and often frustrating. Many of us develop very effective strategies for avoiding doing it in the first place. One difficulty that all writers face is that in comparison to everyday conversational speech writing is 'dense.' The example below captures the cognitive demands made on the writer:

> *Writing is difficult as it requires attention to composing what you want to say and transcribing, that is, expressing yourself in a form that is appropriate for an audience. This is very taxing for many people as it is difficult to attend to both composition and transcription at the same time. Indeed, both composing and transcribing are demanding in their own right. In composing, the writer is striving to put into words what is often unclear, certainly incoherent in the mind. In transcribing, writers have to pay attention to the changing conventions of grammar, structure, vocabulary choice and assess what is appropriate for an imagined audience.*

In everyday conversation I can get over the same idea, that writing requires different foci of attention, in a way that makes much fewer cognitive demands:

> *Writing is difficult, or at least I find it difficult... um...as do many other people. It's complicated ... er... you have to pay attention to so many things at the same time and that makes it feel, well it feels overwhelming to be honest. Is that how you feel? I am not saying everyone else should feel the same way, I think some people find it a lot easier than I do. But the thing is you need to pay attention to composing. I mean getting it down on the page when you don't really know what it is you want to say, that is draining in itself. But on top of that you have to think about communicating to your audience. And you know the people reading your writing will want you to write it in a certain way... like you have to get the spelling right, use tenses properly and so on or they will not take you seriously. But then these conventions change over time. Take, for example, contractions like can't and shouldn't, this was once a complete no-no in terms of writing but in less formal text it now goes on. There is no reason for it to go one way or the other I'm just saying the changing nature of writing is what makes it harder to write.*

When speaking we tend to use more words to say the same thing. We can backtrack (*or at least I find it so; I am not saying everyone will feel the same way*), go into definitions (*composing means getting it down on the page*), and provide more instances (*contractions, like can't and shouldn't*) if we sense our listener does not quite follow us. In conversation, we can also explicitly check for understanding (*is that how you feel?*) and we can use fillers such as *um* and *er, you know*, if we need time to gather our thoughts. Listeners tolerate the inarticulacy of speech as long as the speaker is responsive and understands how to take turns. In contrast, we generally expect writing, or at least academic writing, to be edited so that it is organised and concise. This is particularly difficult as writers have to guess what the reader already knows, what the reader wants to know, and where the reader should be challenged. But readers are separated by both time and distance, and this means that you as the writer need to engage in a continual dialogue in your head with an imagined reader who may or may not measure up to the person in front of your page.

A further difficulty that many students find when it comes to writing for academic assessment is that the models for writing can be misleading. For example, nearly all journal articles follow a storyline: Here is what is known about X; here are some questions that address gaps in relation to researching X; here is a methodology that generates data; and here are the conclusions. This makes for efficient presentation, but it can leave the impression that research is a seamless step-by-step process. In reality, this might not be the case. Perhaps the researchers in the paper you are reading only knew what they wanted to ask when they were piloting the questionnaire; perhaps they had missed important literature and only accessed this after reviewer suggestions; perhaps they jettisoned some approaches to data collection which proved to be impractical; and perhaps there were fierce arguments within the research team about the key points they wanted to make. As readers, we learn little of this because the account has been structured to fit the available space. However, it leaves the process of carrying out research opaque and inhibiting for those wanting to write about their work in a more reflective way.

Not surprisingly, some writers feel a deep insecurity about their writing. As text is permanent, the writer cannot correct an offence given to someone else or edit a careless thought or even a simple typo. This can stifle many a would-be writer. A further challenge is that writing is not only mentally taxing, for most people it is more physically demanding than speaking. Of course, composition and editing have got easier with digital technology, and tools such as speech recognition allow the avoidance of keyboard entry. But, notwithstanding the tools we have available, the production of text is slow and it is rare that the writer gets the speed of composition in synchronisation with the speed of thought.

Insecurities about writing are often deepened by attitudes in academia. Writing is core to academic endeavour, but academics themselves tend to be poor role models for apprentice writers. If prolific in their writing, they can be dismissive of the difficulties of others, and when they themselves struggle as writers they end up internalising the idea that their failure is an individual one or that it was impossible to write given their excessive teaching load. Either way, writing becomes a 'secret activity,' something to be done, or not done, in private and not to be talked about in polite society. As writers we develop, but then feel embarrassed at owning up to, our idiosyncratic routines: *I cannot write without tidying the house first, I can only write in an office, I have to get it down on paper before I can work on screen, my best writing is in the morning, I can only write at night.* If academics could open up a little more about their own anxieties, then students might be more willing to acknowledge their own lack of self-confidence, their feelings of not knowing enough, or their belief that it has all been said before. They may be more willing to point out there are terms that are bandied about (*constructivism, habitus, neoliberalism, post-modernism*) which they really do not understand and hence cannot write about with any conviction. It is not surprising that so many students as well as a fair few academics end up procrastinating, rather than writing.

▶ HOW CAN YOU BECOME A MORE PRODUCTIVE WRITER?

As a student, there are things which are beyond your control. In a perfect world, you will have plenty of desk space, attractive surroundings to explore when you take a break, and access to appropriate technology. Writing is a solitary occupation, but ideally you will have access to classes in which you analyse the structure of texts with your peers and where you can get feedback from a writing mentor. A sympathetic supervisor can help a lot here, one who gives you help in not just navigating your topic but in how to express yourself. Better too if you have opportunities to rehearse your ideas by spending time with other student writers on away days and if you can contribute to group blogs, student journals, poster conferences, seminars, and so on.

If your world is not this perfect there are things that you can do at an individual level to make writing easier and more enjoyable.

The first is to remind yourself why you are committed to writing in the first place. A superficial answer is that it is to meet an assessment requirement, but this is not enough for you to enjoy writing. You need to feel the desire to communicate and to do that you need to remind yourself that you have something to say. There are many reasons why you might doubt this – you are after all new to the field and there are always people who will know much more than you. However, you have unique experiences and unique insights into social problems and your considerable asset is that you are seeing a problem through fresh eyes. Say how it looks to you. Academic writing is generally measured in tone but this is not the same as being unduly reticent; believe in yourself.

Second, be kind to yourself. Writing is as we have seen taxing and you cannot do it all at once. Better to get an hour or two of productive writing done than waste a day staring at a computer fretting about lack of progress. Try to work out what are reasonable targets and slowly build up the length of writing episodes. Many expect to sit down to write in a great burst of energy, and indeed this works for some. However, you would not expect to take part in a half-marathon without training, so build up your stamina for writing step-by-step. At some point, you will get stuck, all writers do, but there are things you can do. For example, a standard technique in creative writing is to set short 'sprints' when you simply get the words down on the page without recourse to notes or reading. This can unblock your thoughts and at least it gives you something to work with later. You could start by setting yourself five-minute targets and slowly increase them. Identify, too, what works for you in writing, at the least find the environment in which you can work best and the behaviour that helps most. Some writers are extremely flexible, they can set themselves up and almost, it seems, write anytime, anywhere. The rest of us tamper with routines at our peril.

Third, your resistance to writing may be fuelled by a genuine recognition that you need to read more and are not ready to write. Apart from reading to gain knowledge of a topic, try to find a text that might serve as a model for the kind of writing you want to produce. Is there a particular article or research report that appeals perhaps because of the way the authors have framed the problem? Try to take apart how such a text is structured and why it works for you. You will not necessarily find such a model in your field, so read widely if you can. A proviso here is that journal articles are not themselves models for dissertations and theses so make sure to access different types of reports.

Finally, any kind of audience feedback is helpful for your writing but if you can try to work with a writing buddy or critical friend. This could be someone you meet, say, every week who is committed to commenting on your text and, in return, you agree to comment on theirs.

▶ THINKING ABOUT THE PROCESS OF WRITING

Academic writing involves agency (your belief that you have something to say and your intention to find the time to say it) but it also involves knowledge of language conventions and audience expectations. In recent years, academics have moved away from a focus on mastery of form (e.g. understanding the rules of grammar and spelling) towards a wider understanding of process. Conforming to rules remains important but accuracy may come at the end rather than the start of your writing.

Process then is the key and while there are different ways of understanding the process of writing, most models will cover and improvise around stages of getting ideas on the page, reworking those ideas, revising, final editing, and publishing. As an example, we look at a piece of writing that sets out to explain a concept, that of community of practice (CoP). (Each chapter has a focus on a particular research context. In this case, the example of CoP is used as it will be familiar to readers in several disciplines, but if it is new to you then stay with it as it is not a difficult idea to grasp. Remember this is about writing process, not the idea of CoP itself.)

▶ AN EXAMPLE OF PLANNING AND WRITING

In this example, I imagine I need to write about community of practice as the first step in a project exploring learning in organisations. I have broken down the process of writing into steps of *planning and rehearsing, drafting and composing, revising, editing,* and *proofreading.*

Planning and rehearsing

Planning for a piece of writing involves reflection on what you have experienced or what you have read. In this case, I am looking at CoP, something which is covered across a range of books by different authors. However, one important resource is Wenger (1998) and my piece of writing covers Wenger's description of CoP in the first two chapters of his book. My first step in planning is to take notes on what the chapters cover and to think about implications for my project, one that happens to be on learning organisations. One such note is shown below:

> *Wenger is sure that learning is not about formal classroom teaching but participation in communities of practice. When he talks of practice Wenger seems to mean something that involves participation in joint enterprises. This seems very broad – he is not just talking about professional practice. So I guess I could talk of student societies as community of practice, a family, or an online group. The big idea is that what happens in practice communities is that meaning is negotiated ('experiences become meaningful through our interaction with others'). Negotiation is not so much about giving up things (I'll give up X, if you give up on Y) but more positively working together to reach agreements about the way that the community works.*

> *A very important term in CoP is reification, but I am not sure what exactly he means! Anyway, practices become reified in CoP. However, I can say that reification is about how agreement is reached about procedures within the community, but this is not just about procedures but agreements about 'social*

reality.' Mmm. When reified, procedures carry a 'thingness.' That helps but only so far.

The next point is a bit easier. Community is defined by 'mutual engagement in a CoP' – community cannot simply be collections of people in, say, the workplace or classroom, or people who share a geographical space. Community has to mean something to the people concerned – its members. I think that is more straightforward. Creating a CoP is a joint enterprise but not everyone participates to the same degree or to the same effect. That seems fairly obvious but important to say. Finally, he says 'the work of the CoP is shaped by external conditions,' if you are a member of a work team there are wider organisational goals to consider, but communities can branch out and have some degree of freedom to set their own goals, they are not simply defined by organisational expectations. That seems to make sense, but just how far can a workplace community go – can it end up being subversive almost?

But the big problem in these chapters is that I find it difficult to think of what we do together in groups (or CoP) as learning as it shifts the idea of knowledge from what is in one's head to knowledge as a property of a group. It feels almost impossible to think in this way. What would this mean for learning in organisations? Would people be learning just by doing work even if they were not aware this was learning?

Planning then may begin by trying to make sense of a resource, in this case, a book on CoP and thinking about the implications for a research project. Core to reading is a continual self-questioning: Have I understood the points being made? What is the relevance of this to my project? Where do I have doubts? As you ask and answer these questions, do not keep your thoughts to yourself. You can gain confidence that you have understood the key ideas by discussing with peers or with a mentor and you can also use a blog post, or other social networks, to rehearse your ideas in front of a removed audience.

In my case, as Wenger's idea of CoP begins to make more sense to me, I can prepare a plan for writing. I can sketch my ideas out on pen and paper – many writers switch between handwritten notes

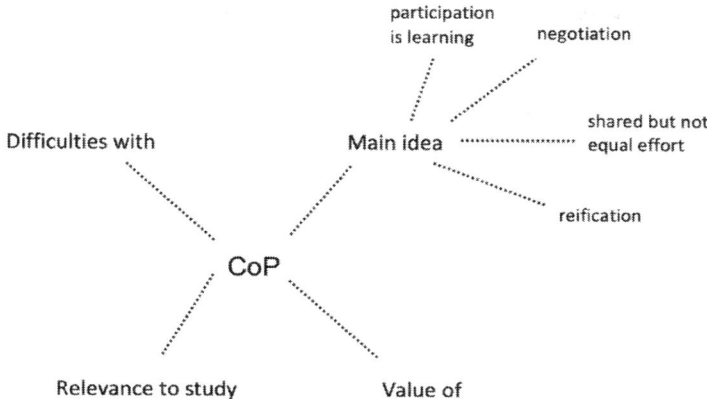

Figure 1.1 Work in progress mind map on CoP

to more formal word-processed paragraphs – and decide on four questions to frame the first part of my text:

- What is the idea of a CoP?
- What is the value of a CoP?
- What are the difficulties in CoP?
- What is the relevance of CoP to my study?

Some writers prefer to plan using mind maps (see Figure 1.1) produced by hand or using general-purpose or specialist software. Mind maps can work well for brainstorming and organising ideas and they can be quickly turned into a series of headers and sub-headers for your text. Some swear by the process of mind mapping and others find it inflexible once the map has been produced. But keep an open mind and give mind mapping a go if you have not used this before.

Drafting or composing

Drafting, or composing, is about getting text onto the page using the notes and frameworks you have created earlier. Here, it is important to understand audience expectations and to make allowance for what the reader already knows. In fact, in writing a dissertation or thesis you have to establish key concepts in a way that is not always done in an academic article. As a student, you need to imagine a rather pedantic reader who wants to know, as in our example, from first principles what a CoP is. This makes your writing longer and more laboured than it could be, but it is an important check that you are not using the ideas second hand or taking concepts for granted. Drawing on my earlier notes, my first attempt at describing Wenger's view of a CoP is set out in the extract below (note this extract includes deliberate typos):

What is a CoP?

It has been long assumed that learning takes place in formal settings and much time and research output is focused on schools and other institutions. Here the teacher is the more knowledgeable person and is charged with organising instruction very often using a series of steps. This has been contested at various points over time and in recent years the idea of CoP is put forward to show how important participation in groups is for learning.

The idea of CoP is that we are involved in participation in joint enterprises. There are many different types of CoP but these are not simply groups we belong to by virtue that we live in certain area, work together, partake in team games or sit in the same classroom. In a CoP we have to play an active role and negotiate meaning together.

We do not simply experience a community we have to make sense of our experience through our interaction with other people. CoPs evolve, members develop agreements on rules and procedures for participation as well as agreement about the scope and purpose of the community. Some of this need to be taken for granted (reified). Reification and community are two pillars of a CoP. A community is a joint enterprise involving negotiation and accountability. Each CoP is shaped by and responds to external conditions, but it also has its own goals and its own practice. It is a communal effort but members are not necessary equal in terms of level of participation and influence.

This draft is adopting a more confident and formal tone than the one used in my notes. Rather than 'go around the houses' (e.g. 'when he talks of practice, Wenger seems to mean a something that involves participation in joint enterprises') in my draft, I simply say 'the idea of CoP is that we are involved in participation in joint enterprises.' The draft makes the key point that membership of community requires participation – it is not something given 'by virtue that we live in certain area, work together, partake in team games or sit in the same classroom.' And rather than get bogged down in the idea of negotiation I simply suggest that 'we have to make sense of our experience through our interaction with other people.' Of course, there is much more that Wenger said about negotiation and much more I can say too, but space is short.

Included in the first lines of my draft is an indication as to how this description of CoP fits into my wider project on learning in organisations. In fact, I was drawn to the Wenger text as I wanted to contrast learning through direct instruction in formal settings (e.g. the explicit instruction given by a mentor or teacher) with learning through everyday participation. This point is developed in a later section of my text, shown below, on the value of a COP approach. I also discuss some obvious difficulties if we imagined learning as *only* taking place in a CoP – even if they were not spelt out in Wenger's book itself.

What is the value of a CoP approach?

The value of a CoP approach is that it sees learning as what we do in our everyday lives and not as a separate sphere of activity that takes place in classrooms, though what happens in class-rooms can be an important aspect of learning, too. Learning occurs when we face everyday problems together and this can be more authentic and engaging than learning in formal settings.

(...)

What are the difficulties of the CoP approach?

The most obvious difficulty in Wenger is that there is too little said about the quality of a community of practice and surely there is a difference between CoPs which are open and outward looking and ones which are closed in their thinking? Should a hate group in which all members stoke up their own grievances and prejudices be classed as a CoP even if members participate freely and cooperatively?

My critical comments on CoP were made in the light of my experience of teaching and learning; it is all very well valuing informal learning but classroom activity, in my mind at least, seems to be important to both teachers and students and not just for purposes of explicit instruction. This raises the question as to whether it is possible to critique a text from a personal stance without having literature as a backup for your argument. The obvious answer is that you can, but clearly you need to offer a more sophisticated argument than 'I don't agree with this.' Instead, you need to show the flaws in a position and/or offer evidence that counters that position. This counter-evidence could be data or could indeed be a personal experience. However, it is always a good idea to search for other researchers who have made the point that you want to make as this will give you more confidence in your counter-argument and further reading will help you put your objection into context. If you cannot find anything in support you might want to hedge by saying 'to the best of my knowledge the point has not been made in the literature but....' Of course, if your thesis or dissertation is littered with 'to the best of my knowledge,' and your list of references is very thin, you really do need another trawl through the literature. In fact, it would not be difficult to find the self-same point I have made about the limitations of CoP put forward by critics of CoP and I could easily enough add references in support of my position.

Revising

Having got the structure and content sorted, I can revise my text by linking the sentences together to make a more coherent text. A revision of my earlier text on 'What is a CoP?' is shown below, again with deliberate typos:

> Core to the idea of *CoP is that we are involved in participation in joint enterprises. There are many different types of CoP but these are not simply groups we belong to by virtue of the fact that we live in certain area, work together partake is leisure activities or sit in the same classroom.* Rather, *in a CoP we have to play an active role and negotiate meaning together.* This

means *that we do not simply experience a community we have to make sense of our experience through our interaction with other people.* Over time, *CoP evolve and develop agreements on rules and procedures for participation as well as agreement about scope and purpose.*

Core to the idea sets out the importance of the link between participation and community. *This means* draws attention to a consequence of being a member of a CoP and *over time* strengthens the idea that a community has a history. There are of course other, perhaps more elegant, ways of organising the text, but the connections are now more firmly established and the reader can follow the thread more easily.

Editing

It is not clear where revising ends and editing begins but at some point, I need to park my concern for capturing the idea of CoP and focus on transcription. In fact, it is a good idea to let some time pass before editing and proofreading as it really helps to see the text with fresh eyes. Looking again at my revised drafts, one thing I notice is that the use of the first person *'we'* to refer to human beings, now looks overused, or at least some readers would find this too chatty or trying too hard to get the reader onside. I could rephrase 'we do not simply experience a community we have to make sense of our experience through our interaction with other people' by saying 'a community is not simply experienced, members have to make sense of their experience and they do so through interaction with others.' If I wanted to stay with *we*, and I find it useful as does Wenger, I could be more explicit and say *we, as members of complex societies.* I also notice at a sentence level that I have one very long sentence that could be broken up:

> *Thus participants focus in on shared tools, stories, concepts which helps them makes sense of what is happening in the community and what needs to be done so that reification is about making the everyday practice appear routine.*

This could be re-presented as:

> *Thus, participants focus on shared tools, stories, concepts which help them make sense of what is happening in the community. Reification is about making the everyday practice appear routine and routines are needed if a community is to get on with its everyday work.*

In editing I have noticed some grammatical inconsistencies as well, it is *help* not *helps*, *focus on* rather than *focus in on* and I have a comma after *Thus*. There are several typos, grammatical errors, and clumsy expressions in other parts of text and these are marked up in an example below. Words that are struck through will be deleted and non-italicised text amended:

Marked up changes to a text on CoP

Core to the idea of CoP is that we are involved in participation in joint enterprises. There are many different types of CoP but these are not simply groups we belong to by virtue of the fact that we live in certain areas, *work* together, partake ~~is~~ *in leisure activities or sit in the same classroom. Rather, in a CoP we have to play an active role and negotiate meaning together. This means that we do not simply experience a community we have to make sense of our experience through our interaction with other people.* Over time, CoPs *evolve and ~~develop~~ agreements on rules and procedures are reached* ~~which~~ *covering participation as well as* ~~agreement about~~ *scope and purpose.*

Publishing

The last stage of writing a text is that of publishing. This sounds a generous word to use for the submission of a report which few may read, but it is apt one. Publishing reminds us that we have to let go of the text and hand it over to the reader.

I have dwelt on the idea of writing as a process as it is particularly useful for understanding what goes wrong when we get stuck in our writing. A recurring cause of procrastination is that we are trying to do too much all at the same time. We are too eager to get words on the page without doing the necessary planning and rehearsal of ideas; we are trying to compose and transcribe at the same time and end up doing neither; we try to edit and proofread when we are too close to the text. However, sometimes writing comes much more easily and we can just get on with composing, revising and editing in one sitting. This is fine though what is probably happening here is that we have engaged in considerable planning and rehearsal in advance of writing by talking to others about ideas or simply daydreaming about what we are going to write. Thus, the five-step model is not a way of describing every writing act or mitigating every problem you may experience but it is a way of explaining what is going on when we write and a useful conceptual tool for troubleshooting blockages.

▶ SUMMARY

This chapter looks at why we write and the joys and challenges of writing. It suggests that

- writing is important for communication across time and space
- it involves attention to both composing and transcribing
- it is a complex and taxing activity, yet some academics take the ability to write for granted
- writing is not a single act and can be broken down into different stages
- writers need to articulate a personal voice at the same time as understanding audience expectations

For students writing a dissertation or thesis, this means

- being kind to yourself and attending to the routines and environments that work for you
- rehearsing ideas with others before drafting
- keeping notes on all that you read – reading is core to writing
- breaking down the process of writing into stages to troubleshoot problems

▶ WHERE TO READ MORE

Although quite an old book in a field which has developed considerably since it first appeared, Smith (1982) is still an important point of reference. In particular, he describes the complex mental processes involved in writing as well as the distinction between thought and language.

Singh and Lukkarila (2020) provide a general exploration of academic writing backed up with examples and short exercises. The authors draw on their own experiences of writing and this makes the text particularly accessible. They signal the importance of reading as a prelude to writing and cover reading strategies, including the SQ3R approach which we look at in the next chapter.

Many of the guides to academic writing are aimed at students with English as a second language. Bailey (2015) provides good guidance to structuring academic writing with exercises for the student to complete. Academic writing is generally characterised as formal, concise, well-referenced, and cautious. We look at this in more detail in the chapters that follow.

In this chapter, we looked briefly at signalling transitions in a text. Further well-used phrases include: *Another significant contribution, In addition, In contrast to, In spite of this, On the other hand,* and so on. Most guides to academic writing will cover the use of phrases such as these in much more detail and a useful resource is the academic phrasebook created by John Morley and published at https://www.phrasebank.manchester.ac.uk.

Murray (2015) has consistently argued that students and academics need to be supported in their writing and notes that levels of support differ across countries, for example, UK institutions seem to have had a particularly pronounced 'just get on with it' approach. An earlier book by the same author provides useful tips and advice for students on writing (Murray, 2011).

There is quite a lot to read on academics and writing, including Becker and Richard's (2007) entertaining account of individual habits and behaviour. Becker and Richard make the point that it is easy to assume that good writers find it easy – they do not. My own interest in writing came not initially from writing theses and dissertations but researching the different perspectives participants, sometimes academics themselves, had in writing in online forums (e.g. Hammond, 1999).

Those wanting an upbeat view of academic writing might read Wegener (2017). She sees writing as essential to academic identity and to enabling participation in an academic community of practice. She offers an account of how supervisors can work with supervisees to develop an academic voice. In a similar vein, Kamler and Thomson (2008) argue that doctoral writing involves identity work and entering a 'discursive social practice.' Both writers have written further on academic writing and Thomson blogs regularly on writing practice at https://patthomson.net/category/academic-writing/.

▶ REFERENCES

Bailey, S. (2015). Academic writing: A practical guide for students. London: Routledge.

Becker, H.S., & Richards, P. (2007). Writing for social scientists: How to start and finish your thesis, book, or article (2nd ed.). Chicago: University of Chicago Press.

Hammond, M. (1999). Issues associated with participation in online forums – The case of the communicative learner. Education and Information Technologies, 4(4), 353–367.

Kamler, B., & Thomson, P. (2008). The failure of dissertation advice books: Toward alternative pedagogies for doctoral writing. Educational Researcher, 37(8), 507–14.

Murray, R. (2011). How to write a thesis (3rd ed.). Maidenhead: Open University Press.

Murray, R. (2015). Writing in social spaces: A social process approach to academic writing. London: Society for Research into Higher Education/Routledge.

Singh, A.A., & Lukkarila, L. (2017). Successful academic writing: A complete guide for social and behavioral scientists. London: Guilford Press.

Smith, F. (1982). Writing and the writer. London: Heinemann Educational.

Wegener, C. (2017). Co-creating the joy of writing. In T. Chemi & L. Krogh (Eds.), Co-creation in higher education (pp. 117–130). New York: Springer.

Wenger, E. (1998). Communities of practice: Learning, meaning, and identity. Cambridge: Cambridge University Press.

2

Showing knowledge of your field

There are, as seen earlier, many reasons for undertaking academic research projects but common to the reporting of these projects is showing your knowledge of a field of study. This means you will need to carry out sustained reading, and in this chapter, we look at the importance of reading, strategies for reading and note taking. We will then look at how to use notes to provide a frame for writing. The chapter is divided into eight main sections:

- Why is reading important?
- Reading strategies
- How to take notes
- Using notes to construct an account
- A short note on summarising, paraphrasing, and patchworking
- Theoretical and conceptual frameworks
- What if someone has done a literature review already?
- Being critical

DOI: 10.4324/9781003161820-2

▶ WHY IS READING IMPORTANT?

Reading is important as many projects are triggered by an interest in exploring concepts raised in the literature. In the previous chapter, for example, we looked at community of practice and you might be sufficiently intrigued with this as an idea that you wish to draw on CoP to develop a research project of your own, say, an investigation into how an online group, a classroom, or a cricket team works. If so, an obvious first step is to review the literature on community of practice, to see how various researchers have explained the concept, but, just as important, how they have operationalised the concept in their research.

However, the relationship of literature to some projects is not so direct. Indeed, a great many projects have been triggered by professional interests. For example, nearly all practitioners are acutely interested in the problems they experience, rather than the problems they read about. As a social worker you may have seen the inadequacy of support for at-risk children; as a teacher, you are perplexed by students' negative attitudes to school or, equally, intrigued by those who succeed against the odds; as a nurse, you have taken part in a social network for health professionals and wondered at its impact. These are all very good starting points for research. Moreover, researchers draw on personal as well as professional interests too. Many a project on family life is triggered by a student asking, 'Is it normal for families to be as dysfunctional/happy as mine?' or an interest in researching online dating may have started with the question 'Are romantic relationships bound to fail?.' Then, there may be something amiss more generally in society that needs exploring and bringing to wider attention: 'Why do some people believe in conspiracy theories?' or, more positively, 'What is the attraction of helping others?' and 'What leads to successful community action?.' The US ethnographer Margaret Mead (1943), asked, as a young researcher interested in childhood, 'Are the disturbances which vex our adolescents due to the nature of adolescence itself or to the civilization?' and this question proved fertile ground for the rest of her professional life.

If our research can be driven by professional and personal concerns, and there is so much to be learnt through direct experience, why is reading so important? The answer is that an academic project needs to go beyond what is personal to you. The role of academic research is not to belittle or downgrade what can be learnt by experience but to throw additional light on social behaviour and actions. It does this in two ways.

First, reading the literature helps us to break down practices which are 'tacit,' ones which have become so ingrained that it has become difficult to explain to others just why, when and how we do what we do. Taking teaching as an example, researchers can unpick the types of questions which teachers ask; the frequency with which students get to work with each other; the language children use when talking to teachers and so on. They can then go on to explore the consequences of episodes or actions in the classroom. The literature provides useful conceptual tools and typologies which it would be very difficult for the practitioner working alone to create. Any analytical tools will need adapting but reading about them in advance will save you working from scratch when it comes to your project.

Second, academic research offers insight into a wide variety of contexts which would otherwise be closed to the researcher. We will of course encounter many kinds of professional and personal circumstances in the course of our lives, but no matter how varied these are, they are limited when set against all possible conditions. Without looking at the literature, personal circumstances are likely to disproportionately influence our understanding. Try as we might, it is difficult not to imagine that all classrooms, families, and businesses are like the ones with which we are familiar. This is not to put academics' work on a pedestal, it is just that academics are providing insight in a different way and for a different purpose. We need to access their insights.

Reading of academic sources is important in order to provide both depth of understanding and breadth of outlook. However, not everything can be accessed, not everything can be read, so where to begin? As so often with social research, there are bottom-up and top-down approaches. A bottom-up approach is a more trial and error one in which you the researcher alight upon articles and build up understanding as you go along. In contrast, in a top-down approach, you have a good idea of what you want to find out and carry out a systematic search for articles using pre-defined keywords. In the first, you are not sure of what you are looking for, in the second you are.

To illustrate the two approaches, imagine I am wanting to research massive open online course (MOOCs). (MOOCs are large, open, online courses which many universities and other institutions offer the wider public. MOOCs provide a useful context as most readers of this book will have had experience of online learning, if not MOOCs in particular. However, do not worry if you are unfamiliar with the context, you can follow the example easily enough.) Interesting questions to ask about MOOCs include, 'What are they?' 'Why do people access them?' and 'Do they appeal to everyone?'

If mine is a bottom-up approach I could, of course, begin by asking colleagues for suggestions on what to read, but my first step is to search for something on MOOCs through Google Scholar (alternative search engines are of course available), and see what comes up. As I scroll down the returned references, I notice something that from the title, 'What research says about MOOCs' (Zawacki-Richter et al., 2018), might be helpful. At this point, I can check the status of the article. This is published in an open-access journal and so-called predatory journals (ones that indiscriminately publish articles for a fee) tend to be open-access. However, by no means all open-access journals are predatory, and in this case, the journal is based in an academic institution (an Open University in Canada), has been going for some time (this is volume 18) and has a focus on a specific field, that of open learning. I could investigate further and check impact factors or look for articles in more cross-institutional or professional association journals, but at some point, I need to trust my own ability to judge the status of an article, rather than rely on an impact factor. In the event, I find the research takes a 'text mining' approach to examine the literature on MOOCs and covers the potential of MOOCs; the nature of MOOC platforms; issues around learners and content; and quality and design issues. The article is helpful for describing researchers' interests but has less to offer about the experiences of learners and designers. So, I decide to read on.

Going back to my list of references, there is another title that stands out, 'The dark side of the MOOC: A critical inquiry on their claims and realities' (Deimann, 2015). This is again published in an online journal based within a university department. The paper turns out to offer a critical discourse analysis and suggests that MOOCs have become associated with an exaggerated revolutionary potential with their contribution framed within a 'neoliberal' perspective. This provides a useful way of looking at MOOCs. However, I still want to find something more empirically based and so my reading goes on…, and on.

The approach I have described so far is a serendipitous one. A lot of research starts like this, with no clear intention of what to read, just picking up on titles, and/or using one article to point the researcher in the direction of another (so-called snowballing). The benefit of such an approach is that it makes the research process feel creative, it is about intuition and good judgement, rather than following handed down formulas. It is also flexible. The topic does not need to be narrowed down to a particular aspect of, in this case MOOCs, until the time is right and, for that matter, an inquiry might be dropped altogether at an early stage if it is felt that there is not much to add to what has already been written. But there is a flip side to serendipity and that is its subjectivity. It is quite possible that certain kinds of articles, or certain positions, are passed over as they do not conform to preconceived ideas of what is worth reading or their titles do not grab you in the ways others do.

An alternative approach is a top-down one. Here search terms are set and the researcher is committed to looking at all the returned references without prejudice. For this, a very broad-brush bibliographic search engine such as *Google Scholar* (or equivalent) could be used but most students will have access to specialist search engines such as *Web of Science* (again alternatives are available). If you do not have a suitable search engine then you could identify three or four key journals in a field of research and search their archives using preselected keywords. The benefit of using *Google Scholar* (or equivalent) is the sheer range of returned resources including peer-reviewed journals, books, conference papers, theses and dissertations, and so on. However, there is little quality control and *Web of Science* and similar tools will return fewer references but ones more likely to be from journals which have met certain criteria in terms of impact and rigour. A further benefit of using a specialist search programme is greater control over the filtering of articles so that more precise search terms can be used to reduce the number of references.

Search engines can also break down the frequency of articles to show trends in the literature. For example, in the case of MOOCs, looking at articles in *Web of Science* year on year shows that there was a mere handful published from 2007 to 2012 but an explosion afterwards with 602 papers published in 2017 alone, though this dipped afterwards. (At the time of writing, it is not clear whether there will be greater interest in MOOCs triggered by the lockdown associated with the COVID pandemic and its aftermath or whether, MOOCs like other innovations in technology, will morph into something less disruptive or will simply be dropped altogether.) Nearly all search engines will also give you the number of times an article has been cited and a web link to those articles for easy access. To state the obvious, just because an article has become much cited, this does not make it 'better' than one that is rarely cited but it may give an indication of what is of interest in a particular field.

The benefit of a top-down search strategy is that it is systematic. You have announced your intention to look at the literature and that is precisely what you must do. There is no excuse for ignoring resources that challenge assumptions or that use an unfamiliar methodology. The flip side is that you may well find yourself focusing on quantity over quality. There is an intimidating list of articles that need to be covered and reading becomes a chore. You can end up reading to simply get through the list without the time to 'stop off on the way.' There is less time too for exploring methodologies or conceptual frameworks developed in other, perhaps cognate, fields and you can become narrowly focused too soon.

The problem of having too much to cover is not, however, confined to top-down approaches as there is generally a lot more written than most student researchers, working alone, can read. The question then that troubles many new researchers is just how much should they read? There is no clear answer. If you are committed to a systematic review, something we discuss later, then you have to provide explicit criteria for selection and go through everything that matches your search criteria. You can only reject articles on pre-determined grounds, for example, where a study duplicates what the authors have reported elsewhere, low journal impact factor, or obvious lack of relevance. If you are going for a looser approach then you should read until you sense a kind of saturation, in other words, you keep going until the main themes seem to be coming up again and again and similar arguments for or against a particular way of looking at a problem are being put forward. Of course, saturation is a hypothetical construct, we will never know when enough is enough, but most researchers will recognise when they have 'got their heads' around a field and only read more as new articles become available.

Both top-down and bottom-up strategies have their strengths and weaknesses, but choosing between them does not need to be a case of either/or. For example, a more serendipitous approach can be used to get a grounding in the topic and a more systematic one used later as a check on coverage. It might well be that whether you are following a bottom-up or top-down approach you end up in a similar place.

▶ READING STRATEGIES

We do not have time to read all we want to read and one way of making reading more manageable is to read with different levels of engagement. For example, when starting a research project, reading is slow; each paper requires a great deal of attention as the concepts are new and perhaps the findings are unexpected. Later reading speeds will pick up. As you bring more knowledge to the text, you may end up scanning more and reading for confirmation, albeit keeping an open mind that there might be something unexpected. The level of attention to a paper can also differ by type of text. For example, a theoretical paper or book that introduces concepts that are crucial to your research, such as Wenger's communities of practice described in Chapter 1, will need to be read slowly. In contrast, there are empirical reports which can be skimmed once the abstract and key findings have been noted.

Reading is tiring. All readers will experience stages in which they are decoding the words on the page but not really taking anything in. To mitigate this, many academic skills courses recommend a version of the SQ3R approach: *Survey, Question, Read, Recall,* and *Review.* How does this work?

- First, *survey* the text. Is it relevant? Scan, say, the abstract and conclusions so that you can see whether it is worth investing your time to read more.
- Second, *ask questions* about the text. For example, 'What does this paper have to say about the opportunities presented by MOOCs?' 'Why do so many people drop out of MOOCs?' 'What, if any, theoretical framework is being used?' Of course, other questions could emerge during the reading itself, but that does not matter, asking questions is about becoming an active reader, it is not about blanking out anything you were not expecting to see.
- Third, start *reading* the text, perhaps focusing attention on particular passages and skimming or scanning others.
- Fourth, *recall* as you read. For example, after completing a section, recite what you can remember and make notes. What you read passively is only fixed in short term memory, you need to actively recall the text to make a stronger connection in your mind.
- Finally, *review* what you read. Here, you need to step back from the details of the text and find out if your questions have been answered. At this stage, you can ask additional, more reflective questions such as, 'Do I mostly agree or disagree with the argument here?' 'Is the methodology sound?' 'Is this an article

I am likely to cite?' 'How does it compare to other readings in this area?' 'Can this offer a model for my own approach to research?' As we saw in Chapter 1, you might also want to blog about your reading – this could be a private or closed blog, containing memos to help you recall key events in your research, or an open blog giving you an opportunity to reach out to like-minded researchers. Alternatively, tweet something – a quick 'praise or grumble' about a particular paper.

The SQ3R approach, as with the five-stage model of writing presented in Chapter 1, can feel a rather laboured approach, and, for many researchers, the steps have become so automatic they have been collapsed into a one-step approach to reading with reading, reviewing, and reflecting carried out simultaneously. However, thinking about reading as a process (and other approaches to SQ3R are available) can be very helpful in unblocking reading fatigue or boredom. Of course, reading will always make demands on your attention so build in breaks, read slowly when you need to, and give yourself the space to properly reflect on what you have read. You can quickly build up an impressive list of references reading one or perhaps two articles a day. There is little value if you approach reading as a chore and get through a large number of texts which you have only superficially processed.

▶ HOW TO TAKE NOTES

Researchers are different when it comes to note taking. Some may make handwritten notes, most now work straight onto a word processor. Some highlight passages or cut and paste from a PDF, and others would feel this to be a sacrilege. Some go for extensive notes and some focus only on the key parts. You need to do what works for you. However, most of us could afford to be more systematic when it comes to organising notes, for example, by storing computer files in different folders: One for the electronic texts we have read, another for raw notes we have taken, a third for work-in-progress commentaries, and a fourth for successive drafts of literature review. It is a useful discipline too to create a file of bibliographic references using specialist software, but make sure you check any inconsistencies in automatically downloaded references and amend them as you go along.

Note taking can be organised in unstructured and structured ways. An unstructured approach is generally more reflective and what is noted may differ from article to article. Staying with MOOCs, the example below is taken from a note on an article (Yin et al., 2015) which looked at unexpected learners, in this case children who accessed a MOOC intended to support adult learning:

Why am I interested in this study?

I am interested in finding out about the experience of taking a MOOC rather than how MOOCs are designed. In fact, I know from other research that online learning is a suspect metaphor as learners are not 'online' but very much physically present in offices, homes, parks, and so on when they are learning. So, this question of How does it feel? *to take part, is an interesting one.*

Next, it is about children: What are children doing accessing MOOCs designed for adult learners?

What was the context for this study?

It was looking at experience of using a particular MOOC (one about palaeontology and what we know about dinosaurs) and researchers unexpectedly found adults wanting to tell them about their children's experiences. So, they interviewed 12 child-parent pairs. It is not clear where these pairs were based but I imagine it to be Canada.

What was the key research question?

What is it like for a K-12 school-age child to learn in a massive open online course (MOOC)? Great question.

Did they provide an answer?

First, they looked at motivation (mostly anecdotal) that children may use a MOOC to build on something covered in class, perhaps as a preparation for college, for general interest, or as part of a home-school curriculum. MOOCs can be attractive to children as they can work at their own pace, access more up to date resources, and feel more 'grown up.' But there are low completion rates (but does this matter?), low in person support, no accreditation, and put simply courses are not designed with children in mind.

So what did the children tell them?

The key takeaways were that:

The sense of teacher presence was lower for the 'child student' than for adults, that is adults might imagine a 'presence' in recorded talk ('the teacher is talking to me') but children were less likely to feel that.

Experience was 'flat,' for a child, the video lectures may be 'just ... another DVD' (that dates the study!). The child could be immersed in the material but more as a viewer.

With family around them taking part in a MOOC could become a 'pedagogical moment.' The examples show how parents can not only explain what is being presented in the material but can use the experience to trigger other kinds of discussion not necessarily directly related to the video itself.

A child may see different things in a MOOC to an adult, for example, visualise the contents differently or treat the online quizzes playfully.

Reflection

This study finds that MOOCs may provide children and youth with learning opportunities that are qualitatively different to school, which seems fair, but I am not sure if different is better or worse. (Perhaps it is double-edged, for example, it is a good thing if playing with the material helps them learn in the way they want, but not so good if they are simply clicking on hyperlinks just to see what happens). This is a small-scale exploratory study, but it does provide a way of looking at learner experiences rather than those of MOOC designers.

An open approach to note taking makes it possible to record what strikes the reader as important. However, at some point, these notes about individual books will need to be gathered together and compared to offer an overview of the field. This kind of *horizontal* comparison is impossible unless underlying themes have been identified. For example, in Yin et al. *presence* seems to be an important concept and I can contrast what is said in this paper with perspectives on presence in other papers. In order to carry out this kind of comparison, some researchers will use the traditional approach of spreading their notes on each paper out on the table and scanning them. However, you can use data analysis software, such as *NVivo*, *Atlas*, or equivalent, if you prefer. These programs are more usually associated with analysis of interview data but work perfectly well for organising and exploring notes on reading. Whichever approach you have taken, the goal is to find patterns running across the texts you have read in order to see how your research project fits into the field as a whole.

An alternative approach to note taking is to decide quite early on what the themes of the research are and organise your notes around these themes. This is a top-down approach, a term introduced when explaining search strategies earlier. For example, many of the case studies of MOOCs cover *contexts, conceptual framing, motivations, opportunities, constraints,* and *methodology.* These could be the headers under which your notes are organised (see Table 2.1), albeit over time some of these themes might be broken down into sub-themes and new themes added. For example, as I read more, I might want to introduce a new theme of *recommendations* and later break these down into recommendations for course designers, teachers, and learners. Table 2.1 is then a work in progress.

▶ USING NOTES TO CONSTRUCT AN ACCOUNT

Putting together a seamless account from one's notes requires, as we saw in Chapter 1, planning, composing, revising, editing, and publishing. We will not cover this process again in detail here but highlight the importance of planning carefully and using your own words to express your ideas.

In my case, planning a piece of writing about MOOCs involved reporting a range of articles. Of course, other approaches are possible. I might go for depth and focus on one or two particular

TABLE 2.1 Notes on literature about MOOCs for students who are not in higher education

Theme/ paper	Context	Conceptual framing	Motivation	Opportunities	Constraints	Methodology	Other comments
Yin et al. (2015)	Children following a 'Dinosaurs MOOC' (based in Canada)	Presence of a key concept	Extends classroom learning; preparation for college; intrinsic interest; and home-schooling	Access more up to date resources; feel more grown-up; and work at own pace	Low completion rates; little in person support; no accreditation; not designed with children in mind	Qualitative (phenomenon graphic) 12 child-parent pairs Large scale survey ($N = 1376$)	Implications are unclear
Reinhardt et al. (2018)	A MOOC to help refugees gain access to higher education (HE) (in English but aimed at world-wide audience)	Descriptive reporting with pragmatic recommendations	Major one is enabling access to HE for those unable to do so otherwise	Format allows access across the world	Refugees may live in unstable conditions without IT infrastructure; lack of accreditation; reduced social support; language a challenge; very mixed student backgrounds		MOOCs not a panacea

Table 2.1 (continued)

Theme/ paper	Context	Conceptual framing	Motivation	Opportunities	Constraints	Methodology	Other comments
Chan et al. (2019)	MOOC for guidance in dealing with health emergencies (Spanish language)	Descriptive reporting	Open course which addresses a clearly perceived need	Access to appropriate material backed up with accreditation, peer assessment and forums	Low completion rate largely due to time constraints and students' changing job demands; design issues raised	Large scale survey ($n = 660$)	Low completion is not a problem if learners can get what they want from the course

papers, rather than offer a broad sweep of the field. Alternatively, I might decide there was not much worth reading in the literature and make my case that this is an emerging field in which the quality of published studies is weak. However, I am happy to go for a general view of the literature and it is straightforward to compose a draft if my notes have been organised clearly. For example, my first draft on the use of MOOCs for students who are not in higher education is given in Table 2.1.

Several papers covered MOOCs for a range of non-student audiences. I looked at young people following an introductory course on dinosaur palaeontology (based in Canada); a MOOC to help refugees gain access to higher education (HE) worldwide; a third MOOC providing guidance on health emergencies. (popular in Latin America)

Motivations for attending a course differed. For example, for children attending a MOOC on palaeontology there were advantages in accessing more up-to-date, visually appealing content and expanding upon the school curriculum. This may have been particularly appealing for home schooled children. For refugees the MOOC provided an opportunity to access subject content at a higher education level when they were unable to do so otherwise because of displacement. Similarly, the motivation for accessing a course on health emergencies was to gain useful knowledge which was not otherwise easily accessible.

There were important constraints on participation including time, infrastructure, and design. None of the papers offers MOOCs as a panacea for education. Two of the papers reported a survey methodology and one interviews with child–adult pairs.

This is a very concise summary. Comments on constraints and methodology need expanding and the example is based on only a small number of possible papers, but you can get the idea. A question when adding more detail is whether to include illustrative quotes from certain papers. For example, the Yin et al. paper begins with a quote:

My dad found out about Dino 101 and asked if I was interested in taking it. He told me about all of the quizzes and work

required since it's an undergraduate level course. He said I
could learn under his account if I wanted. We looked at the
intro together. I'm a huge fan of palaeontology so I decided to
take it. When I first signed in, it said that others can't help you
because it's a thing you do by yourself and it doesn't want you
to cheat. I made my promise that I wouldn't cheat. I would fin-
ish the course by myself. And I did. (Rex, eight years old). (Yin
et al., 2015: 88)

This is striking as it shows a child, Rex, is motivated, externally, through the encouragement of his father and, internally, by his strong intrinsic interest in the subject matter. In fact, it also shows he is capable of accessing a course designed for much older students. Should quotes like these be presented in full in part of our discussion of the literature? There is no hard and fast rule. However, if you do quote, do so sparingly as this is someone else's data, not yours. Do not let the quote stand alone. In other words, draw out what you see as its significance, for example, by saying why Rex's case is striking, and what it shows about motivation.

As your account of the literature becomes expanded it is easy for the reader to get lost and many texts could be improved with better sign-posting (i.e. indicating what is going to be covered) and sequencing (i.e. ordering the points for the reader). The example below shows how my text could be more clearly sequenced for the reader:

Several papers deal with MOOCs for a range of audiences and
these are analysed in respect to context; motivation; opportunities; constraints; and methodology.

Firstly, *context. I looked at papers reporting on young people*
following an introductory course on palaeontology (based in
Canada); a MOOC to help refugees gain access to higher edu-
cation worldwide; one proving guidance on health emergencies
(with a large take-up in Latin America).

(...)

Secondly, *motivation. This differed but most students were able to*
access learning that they would not have been able to do otherwise.

The purpose of signposting and sequencing is to frame a text for the reader but is also helpful for you, the writer, when putting the text together in the first place. However, numerical listing can be overused and the reader, when faced with *firstly, secondly, thirdly* for the nth time can end up disoriented. An alternative is to use other transition words (e.g. *next, further, finally*) and phrases (e.g. *in respect to, as regards, in addition to*). Another approach is to show the relative importance of the points as you introduce them, noting, say, what is *of prime importance, of more limited importance* or, as below, what was a *recurring idea* and what was of *particular* relevance:

> As regards motivation, *this differed across cases. However,* one recurring idea *was that students were able to access learning that they would not have been able to access otherwise. This had a* particular relevance *for refugees whose options for attending higher education were often limited; many had also had their higher education disrupted* ....

A final editing can tidy up the text and insert the required references:

> *A series of papers were identified. These covered diverse contexts: children learning at home (Yin et al., 2015), refugees accessing a suite of course in science, technology and social science (Reinhardt et al., 2018); emergency health care (Chan et al., 2019).*

▶ A SHORT NOTE ON SUMMARISING, PARAPHRASING, AND PATCHWORKING

A lot of attention is paid in academic writing courses to the differences between summarising and paraphrasing. In summarising, your aim is to present the key ideas in a more concise form. You need to convey the original idea in your own words even if you might use some of the key terms that appear in the original text.

Summarising is essential given the sheer quantity of material you have covered. For example, Yin et al. (2015) suggest:

> *Given the self-directed structure of MOOCs, one important question concerns how these environments may alter children's study patterns and habits. An early study of students' navigation patterns shows that children and youth engage MOOCs differently than their older peers. Specifically, when compared to students aged 40+, students under the age of 20 were found to have a more linear navigation pattern (visiting and repeating fewer lecture sequences) and preferred assessment-to-lecture backjumps over lecture-to-lecture backjumps. (Guo & Reinecke, 2014)*

This might be summarised as:

> *One key question is how MOOCs may alter children's study patterns and habits. When compared to older students, students under the age of 20, had more linear navigation patterns (visiting and repeating fewer lecture sequences) and preferred assessment-to-lecture backjumps.*

In this example the number of words is halved but the essential idea still comes over that younger students navigate differently to older ones. Some of the words used in the original (*may alter children's study patterns* and more *preferred assessment-to-lecture backjumps*) have been kept. This is permissible but care should be used. For example, *backjump* is a well-used term in the field of computing to refer to going back (or jumping) to an earlier step in a process rather than the most recent. However, backjump might not be universally understood so it is important to explain its meaning if you feel you need to help the reader.

Paraphrasing has a rather different function to summarising in that it is re-presenting the text as far as possible using your own words. It might well go hand-in-hand with summarising but this is not necessarily so. The example below shows an attempt at paraphrasing Yin et al. in which the term backjumping is avoided.

> *One key question is how children navigate MOOCs when compared to older students. Here one study found that compared*

to older students, students under the age of 20 worked through material in a more step by step fashion. They were more likely to switch from an assessment exercise back to lecture material than switch back and forth within lectures.

In general, paraphrasing works to provide a more consistent voice and to address the fear of plagiarising, that is not acknowledging that you are using someone else's material. However, there are words that cannot be paraphrased. For example, in describing CoP in Chapter 1, the term 'reification' has to be kept as it carries a unique meaning in the context of community, albeit you should still explain the term in your own words.

Discussion of summarising and paraphrasing raises the question of plagiarism, and the more subtle idea of patchwork plagiarism, which occurs when a writer blends material taken almost word-for-word from several articles with no attempt to acknowledge the original sources. Plagiarism is dealt with at length in a variety of books and there is generally clear advice given to students in most institutions. There is no need to add much more here than plagiarising involves passing off someone else's ideas as your own and you should not do it.

A more subtle kind of plagiarism comes from avoiding the repeating of 'second-hand' references, that is, ones used by the authors. In Yin et al. cited earlier, there is a reference to Guo and Reinecke (2014) which I am tempted to include in my own text. Clearly, I should not do so without reading the Gou and Reinecke paper myself. You should avoid borrowing strings of references too. In Yin et al. (2015), three papers are referred to in support of the proposition that school local policy-makers have established links with MOOCs providers:

> *Some school districts have collaborated with MOOC providers to formally incorporate MOOCs into secondary education. (Jackson, 2013; Stoltzfus, Scragg, & Tressler, 2015; Young, 2013)*

Again, I am tempted to include this string of references in my own text, 'some schools have tried to bring MOOCs into their school curriculum (see e.g., Jackson, 2013; Stoltzfus, Scragg, & Tressler, 2015; Young, 2013).' This would be wrong.

Students do not always see why the repeating of references is such an issue. The problem is that you are claiming other people's research as your own. Unfortunately, it is easy to spot when such lifting has been done as the dates of the cited references stop earlier than your reader would expect. Supervisors and examiners are well attuned to the lifting of references and you should expect to be quizzed on anything you cite. You might also ask yourself how many references are really expected. Examiners want to see references to authoritative literature. What constitutes authoritative is an open question but most of us would recognise authors whose work is significant in steering debates in particular fields of study. Examiners will also want to see some of the recent and relevant cases studies and discussions. Excessive referencing, however, adds no value and may irritate some readers.

▶ THEORETICAL AND CONCEPTUAL FRAMEWORKS

So far in this chapter, we have been looking at showing your knowledge of largely empirical reports of research, but you will also be expected to demonstrate your knowledge of the theories and concepts that inform research in your chosen field.

A theoretical framework is the lens you will use to plan your data collection and to analyse the data. For example, if you are using CoP as your theoretical frame, you are likely to use concepts of negotiation and reification as a way of organising the literature and analysing your data. A conceptual framework may do something similar to a theoretical one but tends to focus more on key concepts within a particular field. For example, a conceptual framing for a study of MOOCs may explore ideas of *massive, openness, being online,* and on a more general scale, the idea of *learning* itself.

In experimental psychology and related areas of study researchers are guided by an explicit conceptual framework. This framework is based on past, often quantitative, studies and enables the researcher to define the variables they will test experimentally. The conceptual framework also sets out what is known about the relationship between these variables and provides a justification for their inclusion in a field trial. For example, in one study of MOOCs in a university in Ghana researchers provided a conceptual model (Figure 2.1) based on the unified theory of acceptance and use of technology (UTAUT) at the start of their paper (Fianu et al., 2020). They then showed how this model was used to construct hypotheses surrounding variables such as performance expectancy, effort expectancy, social influence, and instructional quality, all in relation to students' intentions to use a MOOC. The paper describes a mixed methods study in which a quantitative framework took in existing UTAUT models while the exploratory framework guided the identification of additional factors.

It is not always easy to say where a theoretical framework for a research project ends and a conceptual one begins. One way of looking at this is to think of theories as having a life beyond a particular context. For example, theories of attachment, which first popped up in the study of parenting, have expanded into fields such as learning and adult relationships. More strikingly, the theory of CoP has been applied across a great many fields, in many different disciplines. Researchers are thinking, 'here is a theory that was not designed with my context in mind, but I believe it might be usefully applied to that context.' In contrast, conceptual frameworks tend to have a much closer relationship to one field as was the case in Fianu et al. (2020) in which a UTAUT model was used which was already closely associated with the study of technology.

Before we leave theoretical and conceptual frameworks, a key question is whether you need to write explicit chapters on one or both of these in your report. If they have been influential and provided the thread for your study, then do so. If your study is taking a more bottom-up or inductive approach, you may find it more natural to thread your thoughts into a kind of narrative literature review which covers key terms, case studies, and influential theories rather than present these in separate chapters.

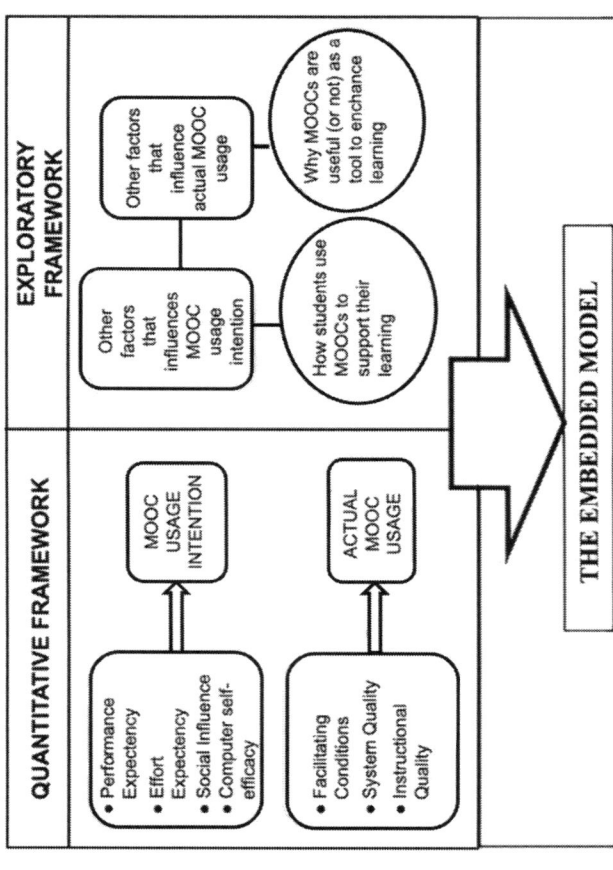

Figure 2.1 An example of a conceptual framework used in a mixed methods study of MOOCs based on Fianu et al. (2020)

▶ WHAT IF SOMEONE HAS DONE A LITERATURE REVIEW ALREADY?

Rather than report on their own empirical work, academics may write in-depth reviews of the research carried out by others. This may take the form of meta-analysis, systematic review, or extended literature review.

A meta-analysis aggregates quantitative findings across a range of studies. For example, if three studies found that being left-handed was associated with better health outcomes and three found it did not, a meta-study would balance out the positive and negative cases and calculate an average effect, taking account of sample size and stability within each case. A systematic review is likewise a review that aggregates the findings from studies with criteria for the selection and reporting of data set out in advance. While meta-analyses are generally quantitative reviews, systematic reviews can be more flexible in scope and reporting, but both can be thought of as kinds of literature review.

Systematic reviews are increasingly popular. For example, the Web of Science database shows a mere handful (39) of systematic reviews on academic writing from 2009 to 2014 compared to 195 from 2015 to 2020. Of course, some of this rise can be explained by the growing numbers of papers published year-on-year, but this is not the whole story. Systematic review is fashionable.

Accessing other researchers' literature reviews can assist in identifying the key issues within a field and can indicate how these issues have been addressed in the past; they can give you a quick and concise overview very quickly. Why not summarise one of these reviews rather than go to the trouble of locating literature for yourself? One very pragmatic answer is that your supervisors and examiners will not find this acceptable – one of the aims of a project report is to show your competence in techniques of reviewing and examiners will spot straight away if you are borrowing too much from someone else. But there are more philosophical problems too. The first is that although systematic reviews can appear to provide objective summaries all reading involves some subjective assessment. You need to go back to the literature and summarise the articles for yourself in case you reach different conclusions; we will always see different things in a text. A second and key point is that while a systematic review may only have been recently published the cut-off date for the inclusion of papers may have been much earlier than the date of publication. Any published review will have left a lot of recent and relevant papers untouched. A third point is that the review may not be giving you what you want. For example, the review might be light on the theoretical frames that really interest you and might have used too restrictive criteria for the inclusion of papers. Good advice then is not to over-rely on a systematic review but to bring in the findings of the review into your account of the literature. Try to avoid reproducing whole sections, you can paraphrase the key points. Be explicit if using a table or figure from the paper, often such a table is described as 'taken from XX' but you need to say whether this has been reproduced or adapted.

▶ BEING CRITICAL

In their writing students are asked to show criticality. This is difficult as criticality is open to contrasting meanings, but it should not be confused with being critical in the sense of 'having a go at' or trying to find fault or blame. Rather to be critical is to have an awareness that other interpretations are possible and that both sides of an argument need to be put forward. This is easy to say but what does it look like? So much will depend on the context and the particular stance you want to take up. The example below shows what an uncritical response on MOOCs might look like:

> MOOCs are changing the face of education. Learning today has shifted from off-line to online; from restricted to open; from expensive to low cost or free. This has been proved in several papers which have demonstrated how people can now learn about anything from palaeontology to guidance on health emergencies, which previously they could not. MOOCs offer free access to the best minds in academia at the click of a mouse. Their advantages lie in the quality of the material and the involvement of top-rated professors.

Lack of balance is in the eye of the reader, but most would find this is a one-sided account of the impact of MOOCs and in truth, it reads more like an advertisement than a weighing up of evidence. The claim for access to learning is well made but this is not supported by reference to the literature. In fact, many studies report very high student drop-out rates for learners as it seems that while MOOCs enable access to learning they offer limited support for learners. The argument is better made that MOOCs are providing new but limited educational opportunity. The example below shows how a more critical account may read:

> *There have been repeated claims that MOOCs are changing the face of education by offering low cost or free access to courses both for both students and the general public (see A, B and C). Clearly, one key benefit of MOOC is that learners can engage in learning in ways they would otherwise be unable to do. However, studies (e.g. X, Y and Z) also show very high levels of drop-out and there are well documented difficulties in sustaining motivation without tutor support. Further, the design of the materials does not appeal to everyone. In short, MOOCs are making a contribution by enabling access to learning, but once enrolled learners encounter several constraints on sustained participation.*

Here the writer cites papers (A, B, and C) to show 'there have been repeated claims that MOOCs are changing the face of education,' signalling this is something being reported, but should not be taken as established fact. The writer notes the pros ('learners can engage in learning in ways they would otherwise be unable to do') and cons ('well-documented difficulties in sustaining motivation') in order to provide a balance. This is backed up with more citations (X, Y, and Z). A sense of balance is made explicit in the final sentence which refers to the opportunity for access and the constraint on sustained involvement. Questions of balance can of course be quite subtle. For example, the conclusion that 'MOOCs are enabling access to learning, but once enrolled learners encounter several constraints on sustained participation' could be inverted to read, 'In spite of the constraints on participation, MOOCs are making a contribution by enabling access to learning.' Both sentences are making the same point but the first sounds more positive and the second a shade more sceptical.

Balance is important but while academic writing is often cautious it should not be bland. When you spot something that looks odd, take it seriously, think about and talk about it, you may be on to something. You do not need to exaggerate your case, and by all means hedge – this will often make your case stronger, not weaker. But when you have confidence in an idea, express it. For example, you do not need to hold back in drawing attention to the gaps in the literature. You can make the case quite strongly that, no matter how well conducted, more or less any past reporting of social life needs updating to account for the use of new technology. You might also claim that research in any field is distorted by the dominance of particular approaches, say descriptive case studies or experimental interventions, or by particular theoretical framing, Bourdieu, Foucault, Marx, or whoever is popular at a certain time, and this needs to be unsettled. Moreover, there may be a problem in the way that research has become over specialised so that interdisciplinary insights are lost. You might want to go further and offer a root and branch criticism of the literature arguing, say, that academic research is biased in terms of who is carrying out the research and in how problems are identified and addressed. At the time of writing, there has been much interest in decolonising methodology, and the idea that research has been dominated by white, male academics for whom English is a first language. Thus, a critical stance on the literature is as much about noticing what is not said as much as what has been said.

▶ SUMMARY

This chapter has looked at showing knowledge of a field and the role that reading plays in developing that knowledge. It has

- identified the close connection between reading and writing
- explained the importance of reading and ways of searching for relevant literature
- described strategies for active reading
- suggested varying the degree of attention you pay to a text
- described some common approaches to note taking

- suggested the use of frameworks to support your writing
- discussed the importance of critically appraising a text

The implications for you as a researcher are to

- use an SQ3R approach (or similar active reading strategies) when reading becomes tedious
- keep both open and structured notes on what you have read
- use frames for writing about literature
- weigh up arguments and show balance
- be confident about identifying gaps and weaknesses

▶ WHERE TO READ MORE

The SQ3R approach has been credited to several people, including an early reference to Robinson (1961). However, you can access active reading approaches in academic skills courses in your institutions and most books on academic writing will provide illustrations and exercises.

Those interested in going more deeply into reading and wanting examples at postgraduate-level might find Wallace and Wray (2021) useful, as too is Hart (2018). Both books describe reading as a critical skill to be developed. Wette (2021) offers a more skills-based approach to 'source-based writing' or writing about what you have read. It is helpful on plagiarism, patchwriting, summarising, paraphrasing, and much more besides. Wette has a useful article on the use of mind mapping – Wette (2017) – an approach which many students find useful for framing a text. Although both Wette's contributions are of general interest, they have a particular appeal to those with English as a second language.

Two very important sources of advice on reading and note taking are Eco (2015) and Mills (2000) who come at it as academics interested in the process of research. Mills is very good on the importance of notebooks and the process of checking data against theoretical frameworks. Eco warns against excessive verbatim note taking, if you are repeating what is said you are recreating the text not taking notes. Eco and Mills were writing before the widespread use of computers and take delight in writing in physical notebooks and in visiting bricks and mortar libraries.

There is a fair amount written on meta-analysis and systematic review. Higgins (2018) provides an accessible introduction to meta-analysis. This has a particular focus on education research but has a general appeal. There are, also, a very large number of systematic reviews in most disciplines. For example, taking this chapter's theme of computer learning, Baker et al. (2018) review the literature on social participation of older adults using technology and set out the process of systematic review clearly.

If you are interested in reading more about conceptual and theoretical frameworks then you might find Osanloo and Grant (2016) a useful introduction, but go to past dissertations and theses too and see if/how different students have used these frameworks in their research. I am often struck how conceptual and/or theoretical frameworks are seen as essential by some academics and optional by others. This is the difference between those who are drawn to deductive approaches, that is they want to have a clear idea of what they are researching and how they are going to analyse from the start, and more inductive approaches, in which concepts and theories are expected to emerge during the research itself. Both approaches have strengths and weaknesses.

The example of MOOCs was chosen as a topic which I hoped readers could relate to. The literature cited included Chan et al. (2019); Deimann (2015); Fianu et al. (2020); Yin et al. (2015); and Zawacki-Richter et al. (2018). I have drawn on the experience of working with my doctorate students, Misrah Mohamed, and her study MOOCs in Malaysia. Some of this was reported in our joint paper (Mohamed & Hammond, 2018).

If interested in software then check out what your university library and your IT services offer. With all software, there is a balance between spending time learning to use reference software and saving time later when reference lists can be created automatically.

Finally, this chapter is not titled 'Doing a literature review,' as there are many different ways to integrate literature into a project which do not require a formal review. However, there are plenty of books and articles which have literature review in their titles and give advice on how to write one, see, for example, Galvan and Galvan (2017) or Aveyard (2018). Both these books cover many of the topics introduced in this chapter and go into more detail on coherence, voice, and the use of digital references.

▶ REFERENCES

Aveyard, H. (2018). Doing a literature review in health and social care: A practical guide. New York: McGraw Hill.

Baker, S., Warburton, J., Waycott, J., Batchelor, F., Hoang, T., Dow, B., Ozanne, E., & Vetere, F. (2018). Combatting social isolation and increasing social participation of older adults through the use of technology: A systematic review of existing evidence. Australasian Journal on Ageing, 37(3), 184–193.

Chan, M. M., Barchino, R., Medina-Merodio, J. A., de la Roca, M., & Sagastume, F. (2019). MOOCs, an innovative alternative to teach first aid and emergency treatment: A practical study. Nurse Education Today, 79, 92–97.

Deimann, M. (2015). The dark side of the MOOC-a critical inquiry on their claims and realities. Current Issues in Emerging eLearning, 2(1), [online]: https://scholarworks.umb.edu/ciee/vol2/iss1/3.

Eco, U. (2015). How to write a thesis. MA: MIT Press.

Fianu, E., Blewett, C., & Ampong, G. (2020). Toward the development of a model of student usage of MOOCs. Education + Training, 62(5), 521–541.

Galvan, J. L., & Galvan, M. C. (2017). Writing literature reviews: A guide for students of the social and behavioral sciences. London: Routledge.

Hart, C. (2018). Doing a literature review: Releasing the research imagination. London: Sage.

Higgins, S. (2018). Improving learning: Meta-analysis of intervention research in education. Cambridge: Cambridge University Press.

Mills, C.W. (2000). The sociological imagination. Oxford University Press.

Mohamed, M. H., & Hammond, M. (2018). MOOCs: A differentiation by pedagogy, content and assessment. International Journal of Information and Learning Technology, 35(1), 2–11.

Osanloo, A., & Grant, C. (2016). Understanding, selecting, and integrating a theoretical framework in dissertation research: Creating the blueprint for your 'house.' Administrative Issues Journal: Connecting Education, Practice, and Research, 4(2), 7.

Reinhardt, F., Zlatkin-Troitschanskaia, O., Deribo, T., Happ, R., & Nell-Müller, S. (2018). Integrating refugees into higher education – The impact of a new online education program for policies and practices. Policy Reviews in Higher Education, 2(2), 198–226.

Robinson, F. P. (1961). Study skills for superior students in secondary school. The Reading Teacher, 15(1), 29–37.

Wallace, M., & Wray, A. (2021). Critical reading and writing for postgraduates. London: Sage.

Wette, R. (2017). Using mind maps to reveal and develop genre knowledge in a graduate writing course. Journal of Second Language Writing, 38, 58–71.

Wette, R. (2021). Writing using sources for academic purposes: Theory, research and practice. London: Routledge.

Yin, Y., Adams, C., Goble, E., & Francisco Vargas Madriz, L. (2015). A classroom at home: Children and the lived world of MOOCs. Educational Media International, 52(2), 88–99.

Zawacki-Richter, O., Bozkurt, A., Alturki, U., & Aldraiweesh, A. (2018). What research says about MOOCs – An explorative content analysis. The International Review of Research in Open and Distributed Learning, 19(1), [Online] https://doi.org/10.19173/irrodl.v19119i 19171.13356.

3 Showing knowledge of methodology

All empirical projects require you to apply methods to address a particular research question/s. Your choice of methods raises broader questions as to the nature of knowledge and the way that knowledge is acquired. In this section we look at

- How do I show knowledge of ontology and epistemology?
- An example: Writing about riots
- How do I show knowledge of methodologies and methods?
- Writing about data collection
- Writing about data analysis
- Analysing more than one set of data
- Being critical

▶ HOW DO I SHOW KNOWLEDGE OF ONTOLOGY AND EPISTEMOLOGY?

We start with ontology. This broadly covers how we think about reality, social reality in particular. Here, a much-debated point of difference is the contrast between foundationalist and anti-foundationalist beliefs. Foundationalism tends to be associated

DOI: 10.4324/9781003161820-3

with the idea that there is an objective world which exists independently of whatever perspective we have on it. In a similar vein, foundationalism can also refer to the idea that there are principles which apply to particular areas of research which define the way that problems should be articulated and worked through. For example, a foundational principle in classical economics is that each person tries to maximise personal gain and a key task of research is to explore the consequences of this principle for people and organisations. Anti-foundationalist ontology, on the other hand, stresses that we perceive the social world subjectively. From this standpoint, we should resist making any hard and fast rules about behaviour and we should not assume there are general principles which frame the way that research works. For example, rather than accept classical economics as a given, anti-foundationalist economists might pose an alternative approach by asking 'What do people understand by personal gain?' or 'What priority do people give to material gain in their decision making?'

This focus on ontology is all very interesting, but how much should be covered in an academic report such as a dissertation or thesis? There is, unsurprisingly, no clear answer and much will depend on the expectations in your particular field. In practice-based research, such as social work, health services and education, ontology is often dealt with briefly while in heavily theoretical sociological work it may be discussed at length. In practice, you will be guided by your supervisor but also by the depth of your personal interest and whether you want to take a wider, more philosophical view of research or not. Whatever you end up doing, we can, however, offer three suggestions.

First, try to focus on your own position rather than waste valuable time and space on critiquing a position with which you do not agree. If you do feel you have to say something negative then be careful not to present a caricature. Instead, try to keep in mind that an ontological stance offers a way of looking at the world, it is not offering a complete description of the world. There is something of value in most stances and gaps in all. Keep open the idea that, just as there are mixed methodologies, there are mixed ontological positions. For example, you might accept that social reality is perceived subjectively, but this does not rule out the possibility of identifying patterns in social behaviour or seeing the material world as something that can be described objectively.

Second, draw out those implications of ontology that seem important for your research. Take a core idea in social research such as social class. For some, social class can be objectively defined using a set of criteria such as income, type of employment, wealth. It is a 'Thing' that can be measured and objectively described, even if the criteria used for measurement may change over time. Establishing that class can be objectively measured is important, as then its impact on outcome variables such as health, housing, and education can be explored. However, from a contrasting ontological point of view, you might argue that class is not a thing at all, rather it is an experience. This makes it very difficult to see health, housing, and education as *outcomes* of class. Rather, differences in health, housing, and education are part of what makes up the experience of being working, middle or upper class in the first place. The social world is not neatly divided into independent and dependent variables but it is created out of a series of interlocking processes which it is the job of researchers to unpick. Is class an experience or a Thing? You make your choice but whichever way you go will have huge practical implications for your research.

Third, consider offering a reflection on why you believe in one ontological stance rather than another. Reflective writing can be a challenge as many of our beliefs are tacit – it seems as if we have always held them – and this makes them difficult to explain. It is, further, difficult to reflect on alternative perspectives if we are surrounded by people or a community of researchers, who see the world in a broadly similar way. There may be quite good reasons why such agreements exist, but take care that you are making an active choice not drifting into a particular approach by default.

If you do not fancy digging deep into ontological principles, then a viable alternative is to focus your exploration of the philosophy of social research into a discussion of epistemology. Indeed, you can generally get away without engaging in ontology, but you cannot get away without discussing epistemology.

Epistemology is about knowledge and how we acquire it. In some research methods books, epistemology is covered by contrasting positivism and interpretivism. Positivists take the idea that the techniques of natural science, in particular the scientific method, can be adapted to the study of society. In this way, it is possible to make broad, objective generalisations about human behaviour and even predict future events. Interpretivists, on the other hand, argue for the distinctiveness of human activity – in particular our ability to exercise free will and to learn from events – which means social researchers must pay special attention to the ways in which people make sense of their very varied experiences.

In discussing these contrasting epistemological positions, try to focus on making the positive case for the tradition in which you are working. As with discussion of ontology resist going 'on a rant' and ending up by stereotyping an approach you are not taking. As an example, I have read theses and dissertations which see no merit in positivism as it ignores human agency; humans are reduced to machines that behave in certain ways because of external influences. However, there is a looser form of positivism that talks about probable associations between variables rather than cause and effect. This looser form accepts that not everything can be captured in a model and individuals are not bound to behave in certain ways under certain conditions, they are just more likely to do so. This is a proposition with which it is difficult to disagree. Similarly, the standard line of attack against interpretivism is to point to the small number of cases being reported. How can you possibly generalise from that? Well, generalisation is not the point of interpretivist research. Small-scale studies provide a lens on what is happening, and introduce concepts for others to think about.

▶ AN EXAMPLE: WRITING ABOUT RIOTS

To see how these contrasting ideas about the epistemology of social research play out, let us, again, imagine a context. Suppose my project concerned urban rioting in modern western democratic societies. Such riots erupt from time and time and aside from their obvious social and political importance, they pose interesting questions for researchers as they suggest that society has the potential to be 'chaotic' rather than fixed and stable. (As with CoP and MOOCs in Chapters 1 and 2, the aim is to provide a context to which it is easy to relate, no knowledge of the literature is needed.)

If studying rioting from an interpretivist view, I would focus on the meaning that rioting has for those taking part and this would probably lead me to interview participants (say, those arrested during riots) and, ideally, observe participants taking part in riots. In addition, I might hope to follow chat forums in which rioting is discussed and, if available, videos uploaded by rioters to social network sites. If I could establish close enough relationships, I might also ask potential rioters to keep written or simple audio diaries. I might begin my write up of a project in the interpretivist tradition in the following way:

> *This research explores how and why some young people riot by drawing on interviews with seven young people who had taken part in the recent protests in a European capital city. The research follows a broadly interpretivist approach that prioritises understanding of the phenomenon of rioting from the perspectives of social actors themselves, in this case young people who took part in riots. Using an interview approach the sense of resentment the young people felt about discriminatory policing and the lack of employment opportunities can be understood. These first-hand accounts further capture the cathartic effect of rioting and the way that shared participation reinforces social identity. The research shows how rioters get swept up in events* as well as *making conscious decisions about whether to participate in riots or not.*

Contrast this to a positivist approach. Here researchers will typically explore the relationship between different variables, or factors, which act as triggers for riots. They are likely to make use of secondary data, for example, court and police documents, deprivation indices, census returns, employment rates and so on, rather than interview data. The relationship between different variables will be explored and perhaps statistical models generated. I might introduce my study in this tradition in the following way:

> *This research lies within a broadly positivist tradition by providing a model to explain the incidence of rioting in a European capital city. The study draws on publicly available data on 352 people arrested for rioting. The data covered:*
>
> - *age, gender and home addresses of those arrested*
> - *level of deprivation index for the locality of home address of those arrested*
> - *place and time of arrest and distance from home*
>
> *The model was constructed using regression analysis and shows how rioting behaviour is associated with deprivation, albeit behaviour is mediated by geography and by social expectations. This research provides a first step in showing a general pattern of rioting. In a follow-up study the model will be modified to take account of ethnicity.*

The two studies are very different. The interpretivist approach takes it as read that researchers must aim at uncovering the meaning rioters attach to their actions. The researchers also accept that rioters may get caught up in riots but they are arguing that rioters are also making decisions, say, by weighing up opportunities for protest against risk of arrest. The positivist study, in contrast, sees rioting as a behaviour which can be triggered by a series of conditions: deprivation, locality, suspension of social constraint. The researchers make no attempt to get into the mind of the rioter but that does not matter, they are looking for patterns of behaviour. Both studies carry strengths and weaknesses, but it would, in my view at least, be silly to argue that in principle one approach is better than the other. Rather each should be judged within the tradition they are working. This means asking of the positivist study, 'How do we know the data are reliable?' 'What kinds of data are missing?' 'How does sample size affect the analysis,' and so on. And of the interpretivist study, 'Are the study participants typical or unusual?' 'How do we know their accounts are trustworthy?' 'What ethical issues does this kind of study pose?'

As with ontology, there is no need to reduce epistemology to a binary choice, you do not have to be either interpretivist or positivist. In fact, more and more researchers inhabit a pluralist world in which they see different research traditions as complementary. For example, it is quite easy to see how large-scale modelling of rioting behaviour can provide a background for a small-scale, in-depth study of the motivation to riot and that, vice versa, how small-scale studies can alert researchers to issues of interest when using large data sets. It too is possible for a researcher to use both large scale and in-depth methods in a single study and arguably have the best of both worlds.

▶ HOW DO I SHOW KNOWLEDGE OF METHODOLOGIES AND METHODS?

Methodology generally refers to the rationale that the researcher puts forward for the application of research methods. This rationale closely links methods to the asking of research questions (RQs) though, to put this another way, the questions we ask may arise out of our preferences for particular methodologies in the first place. Whatever the case, questions are linked to methodologies. 'How many' type questions, say 'How many riots took place?' suggest a document analysis; 'How can I improve' questions, say 'How can I improve social cohesion?' suggest action research; 'Is one policing approach better than another?' might suggest an experimental or evaluation study design; 'What is happening in this neighbourhood?' may suggest a case study, and so on.

Most agree that RQs should focus on the data collection strategies needed for a project. For example, 'What explanations do people give for their participation in riots?' leads the researcher to access first-hand accounts, perhaps through interviews and focus groups, or analysis of uploaded video diaries. 'What does the literature say about rioting?' is of course a good question and one you will need to answer, but it is unhelpful as a research question as it does not point to a method for collecting data. Some research questions can be quite broad and these are not always helpful unless broken down into more actionable questions. For example, 'Why do people riot?' might provide the driving force for a research project exploring perspectives on riots, but better to break this down into more specific sub-questions, such as:

- How many young people took part? Where and when did they riot?
- What explanations did they give for their participation?
- What led them to refrain from taking part in further riots?
- What do they see as the consequences of rioting for themselves and for their community?

In writing about their research, most students will state their research questions very early on, refer to them throughout the chapters that follow and answer them explicitly at the end of report. Of course, RQs may well have changed during a project and some researchers are explicit about how and why this happened as below:

> *I began by wanting to discover the specifically gendered aspect of the riots on the basis that more males than females take part in them, and I believed rioting to be a particular expression of masculinity. However, gender became less important when I could see that those who had taken part in riots were slow to raise it as an issue and were focusing instead on their sense of class identity. I therefore reworked my question over the course of the project.*

This kind of reflection can be helpful in showing the twists and turns within a study, but be sparing. Readers are unlikely to want to follow every change as they will quickly lose track of the goals of the project.

In writing about research questions, some students add sections that cover *aims* (what you are seeking to find out) and *objectives* (what you intended to have achieved in addressing these aims), others stick with just the broader research questions.

In my view, stating the *research questions* is enough in most projects, particularly in more exploratory studies, though *aims* and *objectives* are more usually stated in funded research, when quite precise statements as to what you are going to do are expected, and in deductive studies which begin with formal hypotheses.

Having described your RQs, you need to articulate the context for your research and the population or samples you are going to access. There is often a tension between going for as comprehensive a sample as possible and doing what is manageable in terms of access, time, and resource. Your job is to write about the decisions you took in sampling and the compromises you had to make. Examiners, and indeed the general reader, are all too aware of the difficulties in accessing participants and want to see a critical and reflective account, not a rose-tinted story.

If yours is a case study then spend time not only in establishing the rationale for sampling within your case but say what you think your case looks like in the first place. In particular, do you want to claim that your case is typical of other cases or unusual? Many dissertations and theses tend to avoid giving an answer even when there are background data available. For example, if yours is a study of a policing in a neighbourhood then you can access census data, incidences of crime, population density, and so on to get a picture of that neighbourhood and compare it against national profiles. Often the degree of representativeness of your case will only become clear once the study gets underway and it is helpful to the reader if you can describe how your perceptions changed. For example, you may have chosen to study a particular neighbourhood as it provided a context to observe exemplary community policing, but later find that the exemplary officers have been promoted and moved on. Similarly, you may have set out in another study expecting to see frayed community relations with the police only to encounter a very successful example of community policing.

Finally, you need to write about methods. These are the tools that will enable you to collect the data to answer a research question.

Methods are often discussed as quantitative or qualitative. Quantitative methods are generally seen as dealing with the collecting and measuring of data in countable form, for example, test scores, Likert scales, frequency of events or incidents and so on. Quantitative methods give the general picture, by, for example, showing the spread of opinion or behaviour within a group, and they are often associated with surveys, experimental methods, and hypothesis testing. Qualitative methods, on the other hand, deal with data that are not presented in countable form, for example documents, interview transcripts, and pictures, and these data need techniques such as coding and content analysis in order to be organised and analysed. Qualitative methods feature strongly in methodologies such as life history, narrative enquiry, case study, and ethnography which tend to help describe and explain local rather than general conditions.

As you get into your discussion of methods, try to show the fit between your method and your research questions. It can be helpful to provide a table for this. For example, perhaps yours is a mixed-methods approach in which you are trying to assess the extent of rioting and explore the motivation to riot. This calls for both documentary analysis and interviews as in Table 3.1.

TABLE 3.1 Showing the relationship between research questions and methods

Research questions	Methods
How many young people took part? Where and when did they riot?	Documentary data including police records, court records, and press reporting
What explanations did they give for their participation?	Informal interviews with rioters Social media analysis
What led them to refrain from taking part in further riots?	Interviews with rioters
What do they see as the consequences of rioting for themselves and for their community?	Interviews with rioters

▶ WRITING ABOUT DATA COLLECTION

Tables are very helpful in showing the process of data collection and analysis. For example, Table 3.2 sets out four phases of data collection and analysis in a small-scale dissertation on riots, leading from pilot to narrative account. These kinds of tables should not be overcomplicated. They are a summary – you can flesh out the detail in your main narrative and you can include the full interview schedule, a questionnaire, or whatever as an appendix.

TABLE 3.2 The four phases of data collection in a study on riots

Phase	Date	What?	This involved	Comments
Pilot	September	Semi-structured schedule piloted	Convenience sample ($N = 2$)	The goal was to practise interview techniques and assess the comprehensibility of the interview questions
Main phase interviews	October	Main study interviews carried out and recorded	Snowball sample ($N = 7$)	Schedules addressed the themes of motivation, constraints, and consequences
Data analysis	November–December	Interview transcripts analysed	Transcribing interviews, designing a list of themes and codes, coding of transcripts	Over 100 open codes were created. These were reduced into 7 themes each theme having between 3 and 5 sub-themes (Appendix 2)
Reporting January	January	Interview findings reported	Creating tables of aggregated codes and narratives	The narratives drew on, but did not simply describe the tables

When discussing data collection describe the merits and short-comings of each research method but try to link any general points you make to what happened in your particular project. For example, nearly all students writing about questionnaire surveys will stress the opportunity these provide for getting a general view of attitudes and behaviour of a large number of people, most of whom are at a distance from the researcher. Most students will also consider the delivery of a questionnaire and discuss the merits of online and face-to-face methods. They may wrap this up by noting the lack of in-depth responses, in particular short or non-responses to open questions, as a limitation of the questionnaire method. This is fine but what does all this mean for your project? Why was it important to get a general view? What was it about your survey population that made face-to-face delivery of the questionnaire necessary? Did you learn anything useful from the open-ended questions you asked?

The same principle of bringing the discussion back to what you carried out applies to other methods used in your project. For example, if you are using press or television reporting to assess the extent of rioting you will need to discuss the trustworthiness of your sources. If you are interviewing people arrested for rioting, then you will need to discuss the general issue of access and then go on to explain how you recruited the participants to your study. And if you are writing about the importance of building rapport with participants, then say how you did this. In the example below, a student discusses the importance of location for establishing trust when carrying out interviews:

In my research having a 'gatekeeper,' someone who vouched for my trustworthiness and helped me access participants, was essential for gaining access to participants. The interviews themselves were held, where possible, in a local café as I wanted a less formal environment. I would buy interviewees coffee or tea and cakes and we would cover the questions on my schedule. This environment had the disadvantage that there was a great deal of background noise when I came to listen later to my recordings of the interview, but the arrangement helped establish trust between myself and the participant and gave me incidental insight into the local neighbourhood.

This works but what evidence is there that trust really was established? Of course, we can never answer this for sure, but we can provide pointers:

> *I believed that a rapport had been established and that participants were giving sincere responses as what was said was consistent at different stages of the interview. Further, most participants spoke for extended periods without interruption. They appeared at ease judged by their willingness to seek clarification of my questions and they responded positively when I explicitly asked if they had felt comfortable about the interview.*

▶ WRITING ABOUT DATA ANALYSIS

Once you have written about data collection, then comes writing about data analysis. In many cases this involves the *organisation* of data (sometimes referred to as data reduction), the *display* of data in codes, diagrams, tables, or conceptual categories, and *drawing conclusions* from these displays. In writing about data analysis, it is useful to set out the steps in table form (as in Table 3.2 earlier), or by using flow charts or bullet points.

When it comes to qualitative data, many students offer very good accounts of the process of coding and the difficulties associated with it but are sometimes very light on the actual details. Make sure you provide examples of how data were coded and list the codes in the appendices. No one is expecting the process of coding to be a smooth one so bring in the challenges you faced, this will strengthen readers' trust in you not weaken it. Often reliability of coding is evaluated technically, 'there was a high degree of agreement (inter-rater reliability) between two coders working independently', but do not let this stop you from reflecting on the subjectivity of all interpretation; should two people really be expected to see the same thing in a text?

When it comes to quantitative data again discuss particular issues related to your study. For example, it might be very clear to you which statistical tests are appropriate for the data you have collected, but spell this out and comment on any alternative approaches that could have been taken. Discuss both the general principles behind statistical testing and the detail. For example, if you discuss the minimum number of values you need in a cell in order to carry out valid tests of association, then make sure you also tell the reader that your cells had a sufficient number and, if not, what steps you took to address this. In presenting tables try to ensure that the titles and the table headers are descriptive, and that you follow conventions in reporting data, for example, p-values are often given to two or three decimal places without a leading 0 and if your p-value is less than .001, it is usual to put this as $p < .001$, rather than give the exact value. There is often no particular logic for format of reporting you just have to pick it up from reading papers and following guidelines.

It is quite possible, even desirable, to present your data by collapsing or eliminating categories. For example, if you have used a seven-point scale to assess to what extent respondents agree or disagree that rioting was 'an excuse for disorder' you might break down the data according to those who agree and disagree rather than present all shades of agreement and disagreement. Alternatively, you might eliminate minority responses and simply show those who agree with a set or propositions about riots, as in Table 3.3.

Once you have presented a table then focus on the big idea rather than the detail. Table 3.4 shows data on arrests made for rioting in four locations. When commenting on this table, resist writing that 'Table 3.4 shows that there were 185 arrests in location A, 145 in location B, 76 in location C, and 35 in location D,' and doing the same for each successive column. If you want to provide this level of detail,

TABLE 3.3 Percentage of respondents who agreed/disagreed with two propositions about rioting

Statement	Agree (percent)
'rioting is an excuse for criminality'	67
'rioting is a result of lack of opportunity'	45

TABLE 3.4 Location, age, and gender of those arrested in riots

Location of arrest	Number of arrests at location	Number of males arrested	Minimum age of those arrested	Maximum age of those arrested	Median age
A	185	156	12	36	19
B	145	123	13	28	19
C	76	56	14	29	18
D	35	26	15	34	17

then why have a table in the first place? Instead, draw attention to the key points. For example, you might say 'over three-quarters of those arrested were male and most arrests took place at locations A and B.' Consider defining your use of terms such as a *few, some, around half, many* and *most* at the start of your presentation, to, say, refer to under 20 percent, 20–39 percent, 40–59 percent, 60–79 percent, and 80–99 percent of cases, respectively.

Tables can also be important when describing qualitative findings if you want to give an idea of the spread of attitude, behaviour, or knowledge across interviewees. Table 3.5 provides an example. This shows four codes that were created to capture interviewees' ($N = 9$) motivation for taking part in a riot. Column 2 shows the total number of passages coded across the nine transcripts

TABLE 3.5 Why take part in riots? Number of times a code was applied

Explanation for taking part in a riot (codes)	Number of passages coded (Total N =35)	Number of interviewees mentioning this
Protesting against heavy-handed policing	17	8
Others were doing it	7	6
Felt exciting	7	5
Getting one back on authority	4	4

(note that interviewees may have expressed the same view more than once) and column 3 shows the number of interviewees mentioning a particular reason (note here interviewees may have provided more than one explanation). The advantage of including both columns 2 and 3 is to give a more rounded picture, though be aware that this can overcomplicate the reporting. Note too that the issue of counting in qualitative research is hotly debated and some researchers will avoid it, or at least avoid presenting tables, on the grounds that what is most mentioned is not necessarily what is most important. If you go for tables, they can be automatically generated using software such as *Atlas* and *NVivo* but in a small-scale study, a table could be constructed quite easily by hand.

In presenting tables, use upper- and lower-case consistently, in table 3.5 the labels are upper-case and the codes are lower-case, and show the data in numeric order. When constructing tables, use consistent descriptions.

In writing about the data, reflect on the general idea rather than the detail. Try to imagine you are looking at the table for the first time, what really strikes you? For example, from Table 3.5, protesting about heavy-handed policing seems to be a key explanation for interviewees' willingness to take part in rioting behaviour. Thus, in the example below, I begin my account of motivation by highlighting the importance of 'heavy-handed policing'. I explain what I mean by this phrase and what I saw as the consequences of such policing.

> *The key reason put forward by participants as to why they took part in riots was what they saw as 'heavy-handed' policing. The term heavy-handed captures the idea that the police were seen as exercising disproportionate force in their dealings with participants, many of whom felt there were shown less consideration than young people from other neighbourhoods. Participants felt they were treated with suspicion rather than with outright aggression. In expanding upon this, many participants mentioned being repeatedly stopped on the streets and searched for drugs. They saw these incidents happening at random and as indicative of participants marginal status in society; their dignity was less respected than that of other people. Of course, policing was not in itself a reason to take part in a riot, but it provided the*

backdrop to understanding why young men in this community were open to the idea of street protest in comparison with those in other communities who had had different experience of policing.

The account draws on Table 3.5, but I need to be careful not to turn this into a numbers game. There might well have been issues and ideas in all interviews which were underreported not because they were insignificant but simply, they were common knowledge and did not require much elaboration. The skill of the researcher is to reflect on what was not said, as well as what was said, and present the story behind the findings.

Many accounts, such as the example above, could better come alive through the use of quotes. When including a quote, tell the reader what you want it to convey. For example, one report (Drury et al., 2020) provides several extracts from interviews with people who had participated in riots in London in 2011. In the extract below, the authors explain the importance of collective action, including a shared sense of being against the police, this in paragraph 1, and then they insert a quote (Extract 6) to illustrate the point, paragraph 2:

Some referred to the situation in explicitly collective terms: police were weak in the face of so many young people who shared the intention to riot. In the following extract, for example, there is a "we" that shifts from rival "postcode gangs" who are normally "against each other" to all those (young people) who defined themselves against the police who thereby had the capacity to "over- power" them:

Extract 6

it was just, it was just once the riots started in Tottenham and that's where they first started I think yeah, people my age and that they realised that if we're all united the police can't, they can't do a lot. Normally we're all out here against each other and everything like that, but just on them couple of days we all, everyone thought "yeah let's unite", no one had any trouble with anyone else or anything like that, and that's why people knew they could do it because they would overpower the police yeah. (LON0710110810 [Clapham], lines 149–155)

In using quotes, bear in mind that an examiner should be able, in theory, to locate the quote easily within an archive of data. Drury et al. use the code LON0710110810, but in a small-scale project, you might go for something simpler, for example, a code for each interviewee and a reference back to a log of who was interviewed and when the interview took place. In some cases, researchers give a pseudonym for each participant. There are no hard and fast rules on whether to use pseudonyms but if you use too many the reader will quickly lose track of who is who. It is surprisingly time-consuming to come up with a name which does not identify the participant and/or does not signify something you did not intend.

A second challenge is deciding whether to tidy up quotes by making what the interviewee said clearer. Clearly, you should keep grammatical inconsistencies (in the quote above the interviewee says 'on them couple of days,' not 'those couple of days') and short forms such as 'cos' rather than 'because.' Overuse of fillers such as 'um' and 'err' can be off-putting – though in linguistics and in some more general cases all will need to be kept. You can help the reader further by *italicising key points* and if necessary, adding missing words using square brackets []. Where you have taken text out of the quote, it is usual to show this using an ellipse (…). Your best tool for making a quote clear is, however, punctuation – try to break up long sentences using a question mark or full stop. It is sometimes vital to know where one idea finishes and the next begins as interviewees might be editing their thoughts as they go along.

Obviously, the use of quotes becomes much more complicated when translation is involved. Here researchers often use back-translation (asking a colleague to turn their translated text back to the original language in order to evaluate its accuracy). It is not a fail-safe approach but comparing the back translation with the original text provides an opportunity to think through the faithfulness of the process.

One of the challenges in writing up is to avoid the overuse of quotes. It is almost inevitable that you will do this as you know the research so well. Each quote takes you back to a conversation you had and to a time and place that you have firmly fixed in your mind. The reader does not have these experiences on which to draw and may find quotes merging one into another. Your job is to pick out what really encapsulates an idea or theme and to avoid repetition, that is, having two quotes saying very similar things. What to include will depend on the quality of the quote but here as elsewhere it is worth getting feedback from a friendly reader; someone to tell you firmly when enough is enough.

As with the earlier discussion of quantitative data, it is very difficult to know how far simply to describe the data and how far to offer an interpretation. If you stick to straight descriptive reporting then your text will be very bland. On the hand, if you go too far beyond the data, for example presenting models or bringing in the literature, then you are really doing the job of discussing rather than reporting and that should be a later chapter.

▶ ANALYSING MORE THAN ONE SET OF DATA

If you are using different methods in your study you are faced with a choice of writing about each method sequentially or providing an integrated account from the off. The approach you take often depends on the role of each method in the study. For example, if secondary data was analysed to establish the extent and intensity of riots, and interview data analysed to explore motives for rioting, then you would probably present the data in sequence; the secondary data provides the background, the interviews take the limelight. If two methods were used to get information from the same stakeholders and you had, say, a questionnaire survey of police officers followed by interviews with a sample of those officers, then you would probably provide a single integrated account.

When writing about different sets of data many, but not by any means all, researchers write about the *consistency*, *contrast*, and *complementarity* of the data. For example, Table 3.6 presents summary findings of what to attribute rioting as seen by the general public (a survey), community leaders (interviews) and those convicted of riot (interviews).

TABLE 3.6 Triangulating different perspectives on riots

Riots attributed to:	General public	Community leaders	People arrested
Anger over policing	*Minority view* most believed that the police were stretched	*Majority view* most mentioned cases of heavy-handed policing	*Majority view* most saw policing as unfair and discriminatory
People taking advantage of breakdown in law	*Majority view* rioters were seen as opportunistic	*Minority view* opportunism was a factor but this was not the cause of riots	*Minority view* rioting was opportunist but this was not the reason they took part
Delayed response to first incidents	*Majority view* police were slow to get on top of breakdown in law and order	*Majority view* police did not proactively engage with the community once the first disturbances had taken place	*Minority view* police were operating on too many fronts and were ineffective
Poverty and lack of opportunities in some neighbourhoods	*Majority view* rioters had insufficient stake in society	*Majority view* neighbourhoods were blighted from lack of jobs and other opportunities	*Majority view* opportunities were limited compared to other groups in society
Excitement of taking part	*Minority view* a possible but not a strong reason for taking part	*Majority view* young people saw riots as a break from the everyday	*Majority view* an intense experience, even when just looking on

In the table, the same issues are picked up by different stakeholders but there are some striking contrasts to draw out as well:

> *The table show a degree of consistency so that the majority of community leaders and those arrested and the general public (GP) all accepted that there was a background issue of poverty and lack of opportunity which contributed to the riots. However, there were important differences between what the general public attributed rioting to, as against community leaders*

and those arrested for rioting. The general public believed that rioters wanted to take advantage of circumstances in order to engage in criminal behaviour whereas both community leaders and those arrested saw anger with policing as the major cause. However, community leaders were more focused on the social context of riots, including relationships with police and limited employment opportunities, whereas those arrested were more focused on their individual motivation and experience of rioting.

In discussing triangulation, try to resist the urge to wrap everything up in a neat picture of consistency; there are always tensions within the data to bring out. This is even more the case when you are triangulating the views of different stakeholders with different roles – why should, say, the general public, community leaders, and those arrested see an event in the same way?

▶ BEING CRITICAL

As we have seen earlier, criticality is the weighing up of pros and cons not an excuse for a blanket condemnation of methods. This, we explore in respect to positionality, the use of quantitative and qualitative methods, and ethics.

First, *positionality*. Reflecting on your methods will take you into a discussion of the ways your experience and background affect your understanding of the research you are carrying out, that is, a discussion of your positionality. Very often discussion of positionality belongs in the domain of qualitative research, but it has a more general importance even if some students may resist this. For example, quantitative researchers often take the view that their procedures are objective, it does not matter who is carrying out a statistical test the result would be the same. However, there is no research without a position and the choice of topic to research in the first place and the methods used to investigate the topic, should not be taken for granted; they arise out your experiences of reading and carrying out research, indeed your experiences of life, and your reflection on those experiences. This is where your positionality comes in. Often positionality is presented as a threat and it can be. However, it is impossible to make sense of data unless you have a 'position' in the first place, that is, you have concepts and experiences that allow you to impose meaning on the data. A critical account would see positionality as both an opportunity and a threat.

Second, *quantitative methods*. Many student researchers focus on obvious issues such as response rates and consistency of responses (often measured through Cronbach's alpha). They are careful in presenting the data and in identifying which associations are significant and which are not. However, wider questions are often missed. For example, it is often assumed that validity goes up with response rate when it is more complicated than that. You may get a high response rate for an online survey but if all your respondents had access to a networked device, and non-respondents did not, this would create a serious skew in your data. Such a skew does not invalidate your study, but you need to bring in your awareness of the bias, and how you addressed such bias in your reporting.

Further, many students cover the obvious checks on consistency in survey research and reject returns that are obviously amiss. Perhaps the respondent has claimed they belonged to a younger age group but then later has indicated they have been working in their profession for over fifteen years, or perhaps you have got a series of returns which have exactly the same responses suggesting that they were completed by the same person. Such checks are needed and often discussed. However, at a deeper level, you might want to explore the assumptions that respondents are giving 'honest' answers. More critical accounts explore the circumstances in which questionnaires were completed and judge the 'ecological validity' of the survey, that is, just how likely are responses an indication of future behaviour. For example, large numbers of people typically say there are intending to leave a job when surveyed and that is a good indicator that they are fed up with something, but does that mean that they will in fact leave their positions in the next year? Often the answer is no. What does this say about ecological validity?

Third, *qualitative data* in which issues of trustworthiness arise. There are many ways in which a researcher may assess the sincerity of an interviewee: 'Is their account consistent?' 'Can they provide examples for the claims they are making?' 'Are they prepared to open up about the difficulties and challenges as well as the successes they have achieved?' 'Can we triangulate what they are saying with other things we know about them or the context in which they live or work?' However, a more critical discussion might consider the intersubjectivity of the process of interview. In many cases, the interviewee is seen as someone with a set of experiences to relate and if you press the right button, you will hear what they have stored up and are ready to tell you. It does not work like this. The story the participant tells will depend on the context in which they are speaking but more importantly the story will change in the telling and will further change in the retelling.

A further critical issue for qualitative researchers is reporting not so much on interviewees' 'honesty,' you are convinced that they are sincerely answering your question, but showing the partial nature of their understanding. Students often start out with the clear idea that they are giving interviewees' own interpretation of an event or experience, not an objective account. Yet it is easy to fall into taking participants' views as objective. For example, earlier I gave an example of a study which argued that participants found policing heavy-handed. It would be tempting then to conclude that policing *was* heavy-handed, when this is only participants' perspective on policing. Of course, it might be possible to establish that there were at least incidences of heavy-handedness. For example, you might carry out direct observation of police patrols, or you might explore documentary data, say, records of stop and search incidents, and you could further investigate any incidents that the participants report as far as possible using press and social media archives. All this would give further evidence to back up the interviewees' claim, but the point is that you cannot uncritically accept what people tell you, no matter how sincere they are when they are speaking.

Fourth, ethics. You need to cover the obvious issues of confidentiality, consent, and security of data. This means writing about the importance of making sure that all participants are told in advance about your student status as a researcher, the purpose of the research and how data will be kept confidential. You will also need to explain that data will be password protected and any identifying notes, for example, email addresses of participants will be stored in a separate location during the project. In addition, data are usually permanently deleted at some point after the project has been completed.

In nearly all projects there are some more subtle issues to discuss as well. For example, are we naïve in imagining that confidentiality is achievable? It would not be difficult in many projects to identify the location of a case study, and at least some of the participants behind the pseudonyms, if a reader was determined enough to do so. Then again, in some studies, participants might not want to be anonymised, they may not only be happy but expect to see themselves named in the project report, what should you do then? And what about the relationships you have built up during the project, do you feel you should give back to the communities you have researched? There are some who believe that social research is and should be neutral, you have worked hard enough to show what is happening, you do not owe anyone anything. There are others, often from more practice-based backgrounds, who want, on ethical grounds, for their research to impact on practice. Both are interesting positions and should be explored.

In some projects, there are further considerations. For example, if researching rioting should you try to observe a riot, and if so, how close should you get? If working with children or at-risk adults, how do you ensure meaningful consent? If carrying out controlled experiments, should you cancel the trials once you realise the control group is disadvantaged? These are all important questions.

▶ SUMMARY

This chapter has looked at how to write about research methodology and describe the data you have collected in the course of a project. It covers

- ontology and epistemology as key terms in social research and the implications of holding different positions on each
- methodology and methods and their relationship to the research question(s)
- collecting data and showing awareness of the opportunities and constraints within each method
- analysing data and reporting of both quantitative and qualitative data using tables as frames
- strategies for integrating findings in mixed methods studies
- demonstrating criticality and exploring wider issues in the research process

The implications in writing about methodology are

- use research questions as the thread that runs through your reporting of a study, from the initial design to the collecting, analysing, and reporting of data
- be assertive as to why you are approaching the research in the way you are, but recognise every approach and every method has complementary strengths and weaknesses
- present your account as a best fit; *you are working towards* a complete and as objective account as possible, yours is not the final word
- explore the use of tables as frames for writing, though be aware that alternative approaches are possible

▶ WHERE TO READ MORE

Crotty (1998) remains a helpful guide to the philosophy of social research. When it comes to research methods books, there is much to choose from including Punch (2005), Creswell and

Creswell (2017), and Robson and McCartan (2016) all of which go into detail about design and strengths and limitations of different approaches and different methods. Miles et al. (2013) is a particularly detailed practical guide to coding, representing and writing about data. Clark and Bryman (2019) is a helpful and practical introduction. Most methods books will discuss ethical issues and this is an area in which you need to understand your department practice as well as professional association guidelines.

Most methodologies are discussed in general research methods books, but there are also specialist guides. For example, Thomas (2016) is a particularly good guide to case study, noting the different purposes for carrying out a study, the range of methods used as well as the depth of immersion in the case. There are many useful guides to survey research too, for example, Nardi (2018) provides a good overview of validity and reliability, issues in the collection of data, and ways of analysing different kinds of data. There is a chapter on writing about survey research as well.

You can read more about the relationship between research question and method in most research books, but for more on the traditional view, that is, the questions you ask dictate the methods you use, see Vogt (2008). Bryman (2007) questions this by suggesting that certain types of question are asked because researchers already have a methodology and method in mind.

Many research books and students focus on interviews and surveys as methods but with technological changes other tools are available, including tracking of movement using GPS, rapid diary responses using mobile phone messaging, and the use of social media. These are covered in Hammond and Wellington (2021) alongside approaches such as critical realism, crystallisation, mixed methods and pragmatism which do not fit into the interpretivist/positivist divide.

If you are interested in riots, the following papers illustrate some of the issues raised in the chapter. Drury et al. (2020) looked at rioting in three locations in London and triangulated data from 68 participant interviews with documentary sources.

Haider-Markel et al. (2018) looked at civil unrest and riots in the United States and what different groups saw as causes of these events. They found that racial and political identities provided a powerful lens for attribution. Hart (2018) looked critically at the images of fire and metaphors of fire in popular discourse around rioting.

▶ REFERENCES

Bryman, A. (2007). The research question in social research: What is its role? International Journal of Social Research Methodology, 10(1), 5–20.

Clark, T., & Bryman, A. (2019). How to do your social research project or dissertation. Oxford: Oxford University Press.

Creswell, J.W., & Creswell, J.D. (2017). Research design: Qualitative, quantitative, and mixed methods approaches. London: SAGE.

Crotty, M. (1998). The foundations of social research. London: SAGE.

Drury, J., Stott, C., Ball, R., Reicher, S., Neville, F., Bell, L., Biddlestone, M., Choudhury, S., Lovell, M., & Ryan, C. (2020). A social identity model of riot diffusion: From injustice to empowerment in the 2011 London riots. European Journal of Social Psychology, 50(3), 646–661.

Haider-Markel, D.P., Joslyn, M.R., Ahmed, R., & Badran, S. (2018). Looters or political protesters? Attributions for civil unrest in American cities. Social Science Research, 75, 168–178.

Hammond, M., & Wellington, J. (2021). Research methods: The key concepts. London: Routledge.

Hart, C. (2018). 'Riots engulfed the city': An experimental study investigating the legitimating effects of fire metaphors in discourses of disorder. Discourse & Society, 29(3), 279–298.

Miles, M.B., Huberman, A.M., & Saldana, J. (2013). Qualitative data analysis: A methods sourcebook. London: SAGE.

Nardi, P.M. (2018). Doing survey research: A guide to quantitative methods. London: Routledge.

Punch, K. (2005). Introduction to social research. London: SAGE.

Robson, C., & McCartan, K. (2016). Real world research. London: John Wiley & Sons.

Thomas, G. (2016). How to do your case study. Thousand Oaks, CA: SAGE Publications.

Vogt, W.P. (2008). The dictatorship of the problem: Choosing research methods. Methodological Innovations Online, 3(1), 1–17.

4 Showing you have made a contribution

We saw in the previous chapter how important is the thread that runs from research question to methodology to methods and then on to the collecting, analysing, and reporting of data. We also looked at the value of tables as frames for writing. There is now one more step in your report, showing your contribution to knowledge and in this chapter we look at

- Addressing your research questions explicitly
- Comparing to the literature
- Generalising your findings
- Moving from description to explanation
- Making the contribution clear
- Making recommendations for stakeholders
- Being critical

▶ ADDRESSING YOUR RESEARCH QUESTIONS EXPLICITLY

When you have put so much work into your project, it is important that you not only provide the detail of the findings but show how these findings relate to the research questions you outlined at the start of your project report.

DOI: 10.4324/9781003161820-4

In some cases, your answers will be more explicit than in others. For example, if you have followed a hypothesis driven approach you should be able to say whether the findings support the hypothesis put forward or not. Let us illustrate this in the context of tourism research, a topic we all know something about in one way or another. Imagine that I have carried out a questionnaire survey on the choice of destination that tourists have made and am now focusing my interest on which groups of respondents would be interested/not interested in going backpacking. My original hypothesis may have been 'gender, age, education, income, residence all have a significant influence on the decision to go backpacking.' I explore survey data sets and find that indeed age and education are significant factors, but gender is not. I might summarise my key findings as:

> *The hypothesis was partly supported (see Table X). There was a significant correlation ($p <.05$) between age, level of education and the intention to go backpacking, that is younger people (in the age group 18–25) and those experiencing or having past experience of higher education were more likely to consider it. Income, residence and gender, on the other hand, were not found to be statistically significant.*

It is important to indicate where the data can be found so that in the example, I have referred to a Table X within which tests of association were reported. Choice of terms should be carefully considered. The data may show a significant correlation, but be wary of over-interpreting what this tells us. Age and educational level are, it appears, important factors, but they do not *cause* people to go backpacking. Further, the fact that other variables were not statistically significant does not mean they should be ignored or considered unimportant.

Hypothesis driven research leads to a yes/no answer, the hypothesis is either supported or not. Most mixed methods and qualitative research pose more open questions, with nuanced answers. For example, imagine I have a case study in which one of my questions is 'how do some communities become sustainable tourist destinations?' Perhaps I had found a suitable site, I carried out interviews with local people and tourists and I observed meetings and events. There are clearly going to be a lot of data to present here, so it is important not to get overwhelmed by the detail. I need to report on what, when all is said and done, seem to be the most important factors in sustainability. In my example below, local participation in decision-making is presented as key:

> *In this study a central strategy for sustainable development was the regular meetings in the community hall, in which policies were debated and stakeholders' interests were aired. These were open meetings held every month. In some meetings, municipal officials explained planning applications and transport strategies, but in others local people set the agenda based on issues that they had put forward in advance. The meetings were well-attended and well-run. Local people believed that their voices were heard and acted upon. They pointed to occasions when they had blocked developments which they felt threatened their livelihoods. More positively, they also highlighted community actions taken as the result of these meetings, including a social media initiative that highlighted local businesses and a campaign taken up with regional government for better internet infrastructure.*

The text could also be revised to show where the evidence for judgements about the meetings could be found. For example, if I am claiming the meetings were open, well-attended, and well-run, the evidence would probably be found in observation data and coding of interview transcripts. I do not need to repeat all the detail presented earlier but I could signal the page numbers or sections where such detail could be found.

Making clear statements about findings is a challenge. Many students are acutely conscious of the small scale of their research and do not want to overstate their case. They are also aware that different explanations are possible. However, you should be confident in putting forward your interpretation and not be put off when the picture seems unclear. In fact, it is when the picture is murky that a conceptual breakthrough is often made. For example, suppose I was investigating backpackers' attitudes to sustainable tourism and found that, in general, their decisions on where to visit and what to do were not overtly influenced by ethical considerations. But to confuse the issue, I found that the same young people were keen not to appear as arrogant or entitled when dealing with local people. I could express my interpretation of these conflicting data in a tentative way by saying 'it could be argued that backpackers were not disinterested in ethical issues as they wanted to be respectful in their dealing with people, but this does not mean that they were acting on sustainable tourism principles.'

However, this is being coy. *It could be argued* is an unhelpful filler (of course it could be argued, I am writing the report and I am expected to argue!) and the use of negatives (*not disinterested* and *does not mean*) avoids making my position clear. In fact, there is something interesting going on in these somewhat contradictory sets of findings. Is there a way of capturing the low salience of sustainable principles in formal decision-making *as well as* interviewees concern to show respect in their direct interactions with local people? One possible way to understand this is to integrate the two findings in the idea of behaving *pragmatically*, that is behaviour is shaped by context not moral principle:

> *As regards the ethical dimension, backpackers were pragmatic. They were aware of sustainable tourism as a concept, but this was not a major influence on their decision making (see page xx). However, they were keen to avoid presenting themselves as entitled when arriving at destinations and valued contact with small independent traders and local people (see page xx). This suggests that direct experience, rather than abstract principles, affected their behaviour.*

The final sentence of the extract is an example of hedging (*this suggests*) but this is appropriate as I am making an inference from the data rather than directly relying on what the backpackers themselves had said.

▶ COMPARING TO THE LITERATURE

As you answer your research questions, you will normally want to show how your story compares to research in similar contexts. Here, it can be helpful to marshal your thoughts in a table.

TABLE 4.1 An explicit comparison between findings and literature

Research sub-question	In this study	In the literature	Comparison between this study and literature
How important was sustainability tourism in backpackers' decisions making?	Interviewees were knowledgeable about sustainable tourism as an alternative to commercial mass tourism; they were keen not to seem entitled; they were not strongly influenced by sustainable tourism when making decisions as to where to travel (see findings chapter, section xx)	Sustainable tourism challenges mass tourism; promotes authenticity, supports independent traders; it is growing in popularity amongst many younger tourists (see the discussion of the literature chapter, Sections xx and xx)	Interviewees' idea of sustainable tourism was consistent with literature (e.g. A, 2010; B, 2013; C and D, 2016); their concerns about entitlement were raised in other studies (e.g. E, 2020, F, 2021); there was lower ideological commitment to sustainable tourism compared to other studies (e.g. E, 2020, F, 2021)

Table 4.1 shows how the findings (column 2) in a project on tourism compared to what other researchers had found (column 3) in respect to one research question (column 1). The key points are presented concisely as the detail can be found elsewhere. (Note: You may or may not want to include all your tables in your final report, the point is to use the table itself as part of planning for writing.)

Once you have constructed such a table the text writes itself:

> As regards the ethical dimension, backpackers were prag-
> matic. They were aware of sustainable tourism as a concept
> which captured a concern for supporting local outlets and
> avoiding over-commercialised locations (see 4.2 and 4.3).
> However, unlike other studies (see, A, 2010; B, 2013; C and D,

2016), the backpackers in this study did not claim that sustainable tourism principles were a major consideration when making decisions on locations and activities. Nonetheless, in their day-to-day interactions, they were keen to avoid presenting themselves as entitled and valued contact with small independent traders and local people. This suggested that direct experiences, rather than abstract principles, affected their behaviour. This is a way of looking at tourist behaviour which is rarely reported in the literature and may be a consequence of the more ethnographic methodology of this study compared to large scale survey research.

The comparison with the literature is important as it shows where your study fits. A level of consistency between your findings and the literature can provide a backing (or a level of external validity) for a claim. For example, I found earlier that age and gender were significant factors in choice of holiday destination and if this was consistent with the wider literature then I might feel more confident about asserting such a link in my study.

However, and as with triangulation of finding earlier (Table 3.6), consistency should not be taken for granted or forced. There might be special aspects of the time and place of your project or methodological reasons which make consistency unlikely, for example, other researchers have not gone into the same depth and hence not uncovered the tensions you noticed in your study. It might, further, be that there are few studies with which you can explicitly compare. For example, your field may be a relatively new one and it is too early to draw general conclusions on what the literature tells us – remember here that your identification of a gap in the literature was one reason why you undertook the project in the first place. It might also be that the literature is fundamentally biased, for example, you are looking into race and class in the study of tourism in a way that other researchers have neglected. Or perhaps, you offered a more interdisciplinary approach and you have made important connections with concepts that were developed in other fields in a way others have not done before.

▶ GENERALISING YOUR FINDINGS

A really important point to understand is that readers, or at least your examiners, are, paradoxically, both very interested and not interested at all in the specifics of your study. In respect to the detail, they need to know the nuts and bolts of your data collection and data analysis. They want to see that you can explain and justify the decisions you have taken and that there is a logic running from the asking of questions to the presentation of key findings. This inevitably involves providing evidence that meetings took place, coding procedures were followed, efforts were made to increase response rates and so on. Examiners might want to know why ten and not 15 people were interviewed, what conclusions you might have reached if there were more, or fewer, women in your interview sample and why you delivered your questionnaire by hand instead of putting it online. In short, they are pedantic. Their job is to check that they can trust you as a responsible and knowledgeable researcher who takes pains over your research. Make it easy for them by clearly setting out what you did and how you reached conclusions. It can be frustrating to put down on paper what you think is obvious but turn this into a positive; you have readers who are really interested in the detail in a way that no-one is ever going to be again.

On the other hand, your examiners also want you to step back from the detail and bring out the big picture. They want to know what your study tells them about how we should see a problem, and how we should conduct research on this problem in the future. This wider perspective is core to the way that academic research works. You could, as in our earlier example of sustainable tourism, write a very good report on sustainability issues for a municipality, providing officials with feedback on what they are doing well and what can be improved in the eyes of the local community. That is fine and all the better if the report directly affects practice. But an academic report has to have a wider remit. You will be expected to show how what you have learnt in one context is potentially transferable to other contexts.

There are different ways of doing this but one possibility is to present a model of some kind. A model is a kind of conceptual tool which shows the important elements in a phenomenon, and the way these elements fit together. Whether or not you provide a model for your reader, it is a good idea to draft and revise models for your own benefit as this can help clarify your understanding of how the different elements in your study join up.

Building a model means knowing, or more precisely guessing, what the user needs to know and what to leave out. There is always a balance between providing as close a representation to reality as possible (fidelity) and accessibility (only including what needs to be there so the user is not overwhelmed). If you put too much in a model it is unusable (and models frequently are), if you take too much out then the phenomenon it describes is unrecognisable.

In many quantitative studies, modelling appears in the construction of frameworks when formulating hypotheses (see Figure 2.1 in Chapter 2) and again in the presentation of findings. For example, in Poudel and Nyaupane (2017) factors influencing tourist environmental behaviour (TEB) were explored by means of a survey of 230 tourists visiting the Annapurna Conservation Area in Nepal. The model in Figure 4.1 suggests that three psychological variables (these are environmental attitude, subjective norm (SN), and perceived behavioural control (PBC)), one sociodemographic characteristic (i.e. age), and two trip attributes (i.e. trip duration and group size) explained TEB. The influence of these factors is indicated through the use of asterisks: $*p < .05$, $**p < .01$, $***p < .001$.

Could models also work for qualitative studies? They could do and we set out some steps in the example below. Note that different routes are possible, something we look at in the following chapter. For the moment, though, imagine a study of holiday destinations in which interviews with prospective holiday makers had been carried out. In this study, I found that the opinions of those interviewees were travelling with, wider social expectations, knowledge of locations, the attributes of locations, time, and cost were all important in choice of location. I also found that younger holiday makers had different

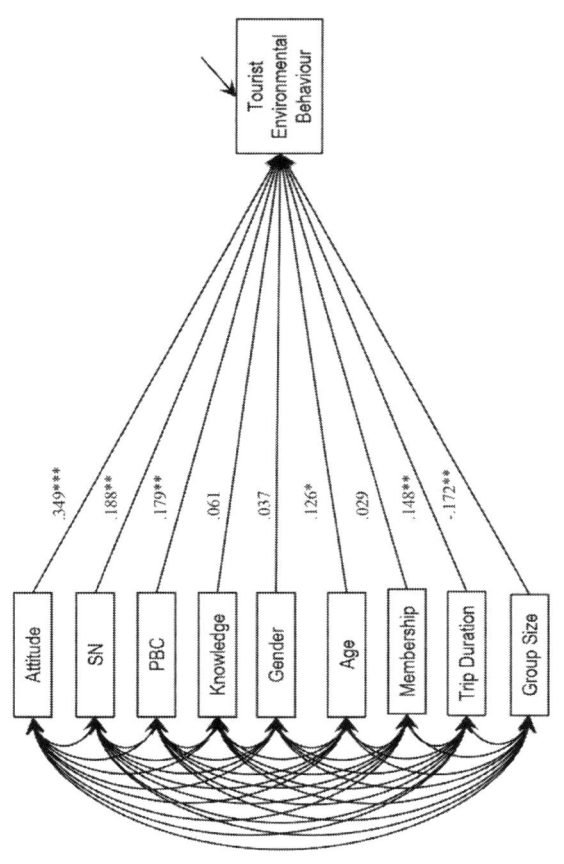

Figure 4.1 Explaining tourist environmental behaviour (Poudel and Nyaupane, 2017: 346)

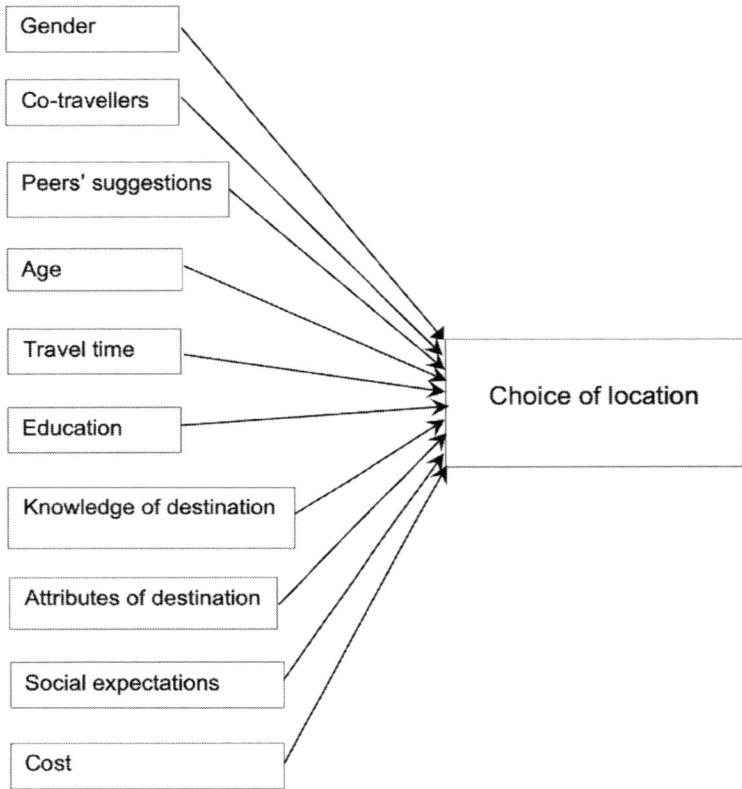

Figure 4.2 Factors considered when deciding a tourist destination

preferences compared to older ones as did those with lower as compared to higher educational backgrounds and males compared to female. I could represent all this diagrammatically as in Figure 4.2.

This, at least, makes clear what was influential when choosing a location and, arguably, makes the process of decision making explicit. However, it is not so much a model as putting what was a list into boxes. I can do better if I tried to group some of these factors. For example, *age, gender,* and *education* could be grouped around the idea of personal characteristics while *family or friend you are sharing the holiday with, peer suggestions,* and *social expectations* all refer to social influences and

I could make that another group. Then, take the destination itself. Clearly, this is important but perhaps what matters more is *perception of the location*: the nearby sea may be seen as an economic resource by local fishery workers but a source for relaxation and water sports by the tourist, it all depends on how you are looking at it. Finally, there is the *feasibility* of actually getting to the destination, the cost and time involved, which makes the destination not only desirable but possible. A second version might then look like Figure 4.3.

This is getting somewhere; I have grouped together elements around larger themes in a way which makes the model more usable. This more conceptual approach also makes it easier to connect my interpretation not only with other studies on tourism but studies in other areas – would my framework work in looking at other areas of consumer decision-making? Furthermore, if users follow the arrows, they can see that the model tells a story: Here are some factors, these lead to perceptions, which are then tested against feasibility leading up to a final decision being taken.

There is clearly more work to do but the revised approach looks promising. There remains one pressing ontological problem: I have not made clear how I believe that these various elements work. For example, without the necessary time or money certain destinations are out of reach and these may be perhaps described as *causal factors*, that is, they directly and objectively impact on choice of destination. Perhaps social expectations are less influential, and rather than being seen as causal may be *mediating* factors, ones which indirectly shape the decision. Personal characteristics meanwhile might be seen as *contextual*, they indicate the kinds of people I have chosen to research. The terms causal, mediating, and contextual can be changed, the point is to think more deeply about the relationships involved.

Then again, I might decide there is something fundamentally misleading about the model as I began by asking interviewees about how they reached their decisions and I seem to have ended up describing the process as a passive one. I might totally revise my

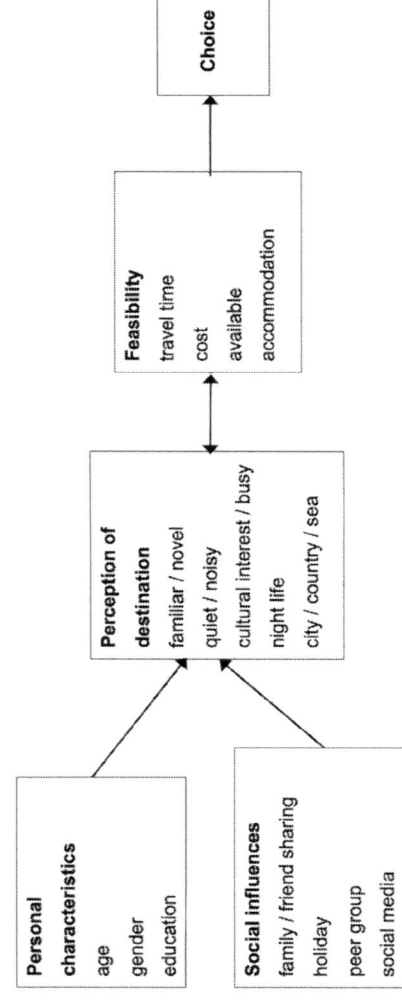

Figure 4.3 Factors or 'elements' in deciding tourist destinations (a revision)

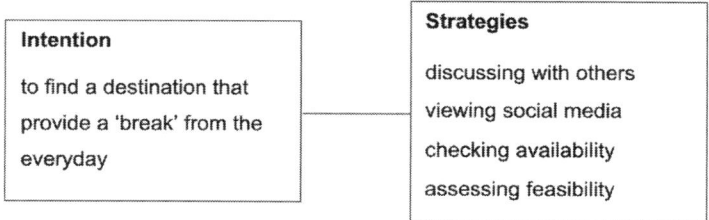

Figure 4.4 Core elements of intention and strategy in a model of tourist decision making

approach by starting with two boxes *intention* and *strategies* and show that agency was core to some of my participants' accounts of their decision-making (Figure 4.4).

Models and theories provide a way to pull out the key elements within the findings and so make the process of transferability to other contexts easier. However, they will not suit every study. If you do include a model then think through how the model works. This means stating the obvious: What do the boxes mean? What do the arrows mean? What is the direction of travel? It also means addressing a more subtle question as to your ontology: Is this a causal model or one that shows how agency is expressed in a particular context? There is a danger that once presented with boxes and arrows the reader over-interprets what is in front of them; rather than seeing a diagram as a way of presenting a story, it becomes the story itself. The model may have been introduced to sensitise readers to the important *elements* in the story ('these are things I would like you to think about when undertaking your research') but soon become seen as *factors* in a story of cause and effect ('this is how humans behave under conditions x, y, and z'), unless you tell them otherwise.

▶ MOVING FROM DESCRIPTION TO EXPLANATION

All students in making a contribution are faced with the challenge of shifting from describing to explaining and this is one of the most challenging things in reporting. Table 4.2 draws

TABLE 4.2 Types of reporting of quantitative data, qualitative data, and literature

Type of reporting/ nature of data	Quantitative	Qualitative	Mixed methods
Basic description	Charts, tables, numbers, and percentages of responses, units of text *Examples:* 15 percent of respondents agreed that …. There were 25 messages sent in 2019	Numerical reporting of codes, quotes *Examples* One person said '…' There were 25 cases coded as discrimination in the workplace	Charts, tables, numbers, and percentages of responses Numerical reporting of codes, quoting of interview data
Interpretative description	The key take-aways within the data are identified *Examples* Most respondents found lack of time was a problem, this was extenuated by … More messages were sent to an online forum in the first half of the discussion than the second	The key take-aways within the data are identified, any direct quotes are contextualised *Example* A key concern for most participants was racial stereotyping. One participant explained "…"	The key take-aways within the different sets of data are identified, and triangulated *Examples* A key concern for most students was the delivery of online learning. However, teachers had a contrasting perspective… The picture built up from the survey data is reinforced in the light of other data

Type of reporting/ nature of data	Quantitative	Qualitative	Mixed methods
Analytical description	The relationship between different findings or factors are drawn out, often in tables or models *Examples* There was a significant correlation between X and Y This model shows the following factors are important when it comes to decision making	Key ideas and concepts are used to integrate findings *Example* The concept of pragmatism captures many of strategies used by participants. Pragmatism explains a commitment to greater equity but also the limits on the commitment to equity	Models and/or key concepts are used to integrate different sets of findings *Example* There was significant relationship between X and Y. in the survey data and this association was mirrored in the interview data. Both sets of data suggested that resilience was a valuable way to understand participants' perspectives
Explanation	The reasons for relationships within models or tables are given *Example* The model can be explained by the previously reported close association between class and outcome …	The reasons for concepts and explaining how they worked *Example* The idea of a pragmatic response captures the idea that workers were supportive of trade unionism when it protected their immediate interests, but were less interested in wider goals	The reasons for relationships and/ or concepts are given *Example* The idea of resilience works well to explain participant behaviour in this study because it captures personal characteristics (person x is resilient) *as well as* contextual support (this institution nurtures resilience) …

Table 4.2 (continued)

Type of reporting/ nature of data	Quantitative	Qualitative	Mixed methods
Theoretical explanation	Evokes concepts from the literature to explain relationships Epistemological assumptions discussed *Example* A theoretical backing for this model lies not only in the empirical literature on class and outcome but also in the more abstract work on economic, social, and cultural capital in Bourdieu. The model provided should not be seen as predictive – class does not cause certain outcomes – rather it increases the odds of such outcomes	Evokes and adapts concepts from the literature to explain relationships Epistemological assumptions discussed New concepts introduced *Examples* The idea of alienation in this study is informed by work by Durkheim, but differs in respect to … Although workers felt they lacked agency at work, they also gave examples when they could exercise control over their tasks	Evokes and adapts concepts from the literature to explain relationships Epistemological assumptions discussed *Example* The concept of resilience in the literature has shifted from a focus on individuals to a wider focus on individuals in context. This is supported in this study; resilience is not the sole responsibility of the individual

together our previous discussion and shows different types of reporting in respect to quantitative, qualitative, and mixed methods research. Thus, that at times you may be providing a *basic description*, these are simple statements of what you found or what people had said. However, as discussed earlier (pages 63–69), there is value in a more *interpretative description*, one which draws attention to patterns within the data while staying close to the data itself. Next, at a further level of abstraction, you might provide an *analytical description* which shows the relationship between the elements in your study and the way these elements work together to produce an outcome. This might be achieved by introducing conceptual categories (such as pragmatic adjustment, page 82) or by models (pages 85–91) and analytical descriptions (e.g. thick description which aims to show the meaning of an event from the participants perspective, see a later example on pages 133–5).

Analytic description may be a point at which many dissertations stop, but there is something missing if your report is not doing the work of *explaining* and *theorising*. These words mean different things in different contexts. In quantitative work, explanation means going beyond the identification of a significant association between X and Y, rather you need to say why X is related to Y or why a model works as it does. We see an example of explanation later on in Chapter 5 in a study of the gender pay gap in the IT industry (Segovia-Pérez et al., 2020). Here the authors offer an explanation for discrimination when it comes to renumeration in terms of cultural stereotyping (see page 128). There are of course other possible explanations in this and in any other study, but researchers need to be brave enough to step back from the data and offer a way of understanding the data even if what they offer is a best fit. In the same section (pages 129–130), we look at another example (Scott-Arthur et al., 2021) of how a particular theory associated with the French sociologist Bourdieu was used to explain to throw light on inequalities, ones associated with lifestyle. Theories need not, of course, be sociological but in this case, Bourdieu was helpful as he is not only offering a theory of social stratification but a theory of why people act in the way that they do and the nature of their agency.

Tables, such as Table 4.2 above, help to explain the different kinds of writing that you are expected to carry out when writing a report. However, this table needs to be interpreted flexibly for two main reasons.

First, faced with a typology it is tempting to conclude that there is a clear break from one type of reporting to the next. But in practice it is very difficult to say where, for example, explanation ends and theoretical explanation begins. Rather than try to place everything you write in one box or another try instead to think about where your reporting best fits along a continuum from description to explanation. If it is mostly at one end of this continuum there might be a problem to address. However, bear in mind that the extent of the problem can only be understood in the context of the field of study. For example, there are contexts in which descriptive reporting serves a particularly useful purpose as they are new and under-reported, while there are other contexts in which descriptive reporting is laboured and unnecessary.

Secondly, typologies such as the one I have offered are often viewed as a hierarchy: the first and easiest rung of the ladder is describing, the last, the most elevated and difficult step to take is providing theoretical explanation. Explanation is then better than description. I do not think that is right. Simple basic description of the type 'X said this, Y said that and Z said something else altogether' is simplistic and not exactly stretching, but there are others kinds of description which are much more challenging. In particular, writing interpretative description requires patience and attention to detail, and is an important step on the way to explaining. In the same vein, analytical description is a key outcome of any study and there is, as we see later, a distinctive kind of approach, thick description, which offers both explanation and description in a seamless text.

▶ MAKING THE CONTRIBUTION CLEAR

It is often difficult to find the confidence to finish a dissertation or thesis by claiming a contribution to knowledge. There is, after all, so much already written, and anyway your study is small-scale and perhaps there were aspects of the data analysis or interpretation you were not so certain of. But do try to get into a different mindset. Focus on the big picture. A way of rehearsing for this is to ask yourself, or better to have someone ask you, 'What have you found out and why was this important?' Give yourself two minutes to answer. You will probably find it difficult first time around, so record your attempts and reflect on what you said as you play back your recording.

What kinds of claims might you make? First, you may make a theoretical claim. For example, you used a particularly new and innovative framework that had not be used before to guide your study, or you followed a bottom-up approach and developed conceptual categories that were quite original. Perhaps you succeeded in offering a new perspective – decision making had largely been seen in behavioural terms rather than as an expression of the agency, or vice versa. Or your theoretical claim might be more limited, your contribution was to show the value of testing an existing framework in a new context, or to adapt a framework from a different field. This sounds modest as a claim but it could represent an important contribution to knowledge.

In writing about your theoretical contribution, you should address the generalisability of your model or conceptual contribution. At one end of the spectrum, you may claim that what you have found is of general significance, that you have modelled a relationship between, say, factors of cost, distance and climate, and holiday makers' choice of destination that is predictive, that is, it can be expected to operate in any situation you care to choose, rather as a general law of physics might show the application of heat on metal anywhere, any time. To go down this route you need the evidence of a significant association between variables, but you would also need to provide a wider backing as to why (a) these two or more variables should be associated and (b) the direction of influence of A on B, not B on A. In other words, what do you know from other studies that backs up and explains what you have found? If you wanted to go further and claim that your explanation of an event or a behaviour really is better and more universal than anyone else's then you would need to show the shortcomings in other work and perhaps argue that all behaviour really was predictable, the inevitable consequence of cause and effect. Good luck with that one.

At the other end of the spectrum, you may want to reject the idea of generalisability completely. What you presented was interesting but local; there was very little likelihood of seeing the same conditions being replicated elsewhere. Of course, this is a defensible position, but bear in mind that readers may end up quite disappointed to have read your account only to find it has no relevance to the worlds they inhabit and study. A way to address this is to write about the relatability of your study. Your contribution is then one of helping others think about a phenomenon in new ways. It is up to readers to decide if this contribution is helpful but at the least make it easy for them to judge whether it is and get them thinking.

A second kind of contribution is a methodological one. Indeed, there is nearly always something about your research design to which you should draw attention. Perhaps your study employed a mixed method research design, with a particularly subtle triangulation strategy, when such an approach is unusual; it may have been a qualitative study in a field dominated by quantitative methods, or vice versa; you had a close relationship with participants and your finding were particularly trustworthy; you used social media data in a way that was not possible in the past. And even though your study was a snapshot taken at a particular point in time you did try to follow up your participants, in ways that most studies simply had not done.

Third, you may want to make the point that your study contributes by addressing a particularly important issue that is facing the world. For example, the choice of sustainable tourism as a topic speaks to a wider concern for the environment that is not just a local issue but a world issue. Be clear, however, that your study, unless you are working in an action research tradition, is really proposing a way of looking at a problem, it is not trying to make a direct contribution in itself. What you hope to do is contribute to the way a problem is discussed.

Fourth, there is always something about your particular context to which it is worth drawing attention. Perhaps there have been sustainable tourism studies before but nothing undertaken in the country, region or even locality that you are writing about. Likewise, there is something about the timing of your study that might be important, for example, it was undertaken at the time of COVID lockdown, or when there was significant economic contraction/growth in a sector, or it showed the importance of technology in a way which make previous studies seem dated.

▶ MAKING RECOMMENDATIONS

Ideas differ about how far to go with recommendations. For some, the point of academic research is to describe what is happening and it is not the job of researchers to draw conclusions, policy makers, practitioners, and readers in general need to work those out for themselves. For others, recommendations are important, you are making no more than suggestions, but you know a lot about the context and you have advice to give.

You need to reach your own decision on this, but my view is that it is not only reasonable but expected that you make some recommendations. However, resist telling people what they *should* do as, first, you are in no position to order them about and second, you may not have the full picture of the contexts in which they are working. Couch your language appropriately and be clear as to whom your recommendations are directed. If, as earlier, you have something to say about sustainable tourism, then your audience might be tourists themselves, independent traders, municipalities, and fellow researchers and you may address your recommendations to each in turn:

> For travellers: *Consider actively choosing locations which have a commitment to sustainable tourism and during your stay support independent, local traders where possible. You can find the required information from social networks, local tourist offices, and by word of mouth.*

For municipalities: *Try to enlist the local community in promoting and sustaining your region as a destination. Invest in local tourism offices and make active attempts to ensure all local traders are represented in web sites and literature. Try to be proactive in enlisting community organisations, do not wait for them to contact you. Being sustainable does not rule out larger scale operations but think through the implications of any decisions about tourist development that you make. Invite community feedback.*

For small traders and hosts: *Consider how you can present your offer to the tourists you want to attract. Work together where there are gains from economies of scale, for example share the cost of advertising and training. Support other local traders when you cannot cater for a tourist yourself.*

For not-for-profit organisations: *Continue to involve local people in decision making. Consider offering classes that will help local people to interact and sell services to tourists.*

For other researchers interested in this field: *Immerse yourself in the literature but identify gaps, for example gaps in methodology, gaps in accounts written with or by local people. Try to keep a critical perspective, do not assume that one pattern of sustainable tourism is either desirable or attainable. Be aware of the way tourism is changing with the use of social media and draw on creative methods in the exploration of your research questions.*

▶ BEING CRITICAL

A critical approach is one in which you state your views but accept there are other ways of looking at the problem. Being critical is about supporting claims with evidence but also showing how and why this evidence is relevant and trustworthy. Commentators on social science sometimes veer between two extremes: An excessive faith in the objectivity of findings and a root and branch questioning as to whether objectivity of any kind exists. There is a middle way in which you, as researcher, put forward arguments, back those arguments up, but recognise your limitations. By drawing attention to these limitations, you often strengthen your argument rather than weaken it. Indeed, readers will begin to lose trust in you as they find you out, for example, when they notice that you have ignored certain literature or you are over-confident in stating the validity of your coding framework. In contrast, if you stay ahead of the reader and raise the problems of interpretation before the reader spots them, then trust is strengthened. Of course, if you raise a problem then you need to say how this problem happened, what you did to address it and what you might do about it next time. In the example below, a student discusses low response rates:

> One limitation was the response rate. I increased response rate through sending out a couple of reminders, but I could not send more reminders than that due to ethical concerns. Although the final response rate was sufficient to test for the key hypotheses, I needed in some cases to collapse groups in order to carry out reliable tests. For example, I divided respondents between older and younger groups rather than use the five groups I had intended to. If doing the study again I might use social media to promote interest in the study and take more steps to stress the value of the study for stakeholders.

In this further example, a student discusses how their understanding of the nature of their case changed over the course of the project:

> My case study was selected to represent best practice in community involvement and although good practice was often observed there were shortcomings I had not predicted. In the end what I saw was not exemplary but rather what was good but not altogether untypical of the sector as a whole, based on wider reporting. This does not invalidate my study. A typical or 'key' case can be as important as an exemplary or unusual case. Moreover, my findings clearly throw light on what exemplary practice looks like and should look like. However, this tension between the case as it was and the case as I had first imagined was one I needed to address throughout the study.

There are challenges and limitations in all studies, it is whether you notice them and how you take account of them that matters.

▶ SUMMARY

This chapter has covered

- addressing your research questions clearly and assertively when reporting on findings
- using models, concepts, and frames to make your findings relatable/transferable to researchers in other contexts
- offering different types of theoretical contributions your research can make
- spelling out the implications of your research for different audiences.

The implications in writing about your contribution are

- make clear what you have found out and why this is important
- pull out the key elements of factors which create the events or experiences you are describing
- be assertive when offering interpretations but accept that there are other ways of seeing the data
- address the 'so what?' Draw out the implications of your research for different audiences

▶ WHERE TO READ MORE

Many of the research books mentioned at the end of the previous chapter discuss research design and questions of validity, reliability, and trustworthiness. In addition, Coolican (2017) provides a guide to the quantitative project in psychology and has a useful chapter on report writing. If you want to take an explicitly statistical approach to modelling, then there are many books to choose from. For example, Keith (2019) starts from bivariate regression (relationships between two variables), goes on to multiple regression (analysis of the influence of several variables on outcomes) and then to structural equation modelling (a term used to refer to a range of approaches which set to evaluate the fit between theoretical models and observed data). In the qualitative tradition,

Strauss and Corbin (1990) provide a grounded, or bottom-up, guide to coding, theorising, and drawing conclusions from the data in general. They discuss the diagrammatic representation of findings, too.

In respect to theory and theorising, Krause (2016) and earlier Abend (2008) have stressed that the term theory covers a variety of meanings including showing associations between variables; providing a picture as to how data fit together; using existing theories in new contexts; creating new concepts. This chapter has only touched the surface and in a further paper, I argue that theorising is under researched and requires a different way of thinking (Hammond, 2018).

If you are interested in typologies you might want to look at Bloom's taxonomy which identifies lower order to higher functions in teaching, learning, and assessment. The taxonomy covers six categories: remembering, understanding, applying, analysing, evaluating, and creating. It has been used in teaching, learning and assessment of academic writing (e.g. Al-Hammadi and Sidek, 2015) though coming in and out of favour at different times. As an alternative, Wilmot (2021) provides a detailed analysis of a student's writing on attitudes to climate change as it shifted from descriptive to theoretical.

The discussion of tourism in this chapter was there to show the kinds of debates academics have, it was not based on a specific research project. However, I found the several tourism studies useful for illustrating methodologies, including: Bandyopadhyay and Patil (2017) which looked at volunteer tourism from a 'decolonising feminist perspective; Haddouche & Salomone (2018) which explored young people's ('generation z') attitudes to tourism; Kim et al. (2019), in which social network data was used to explore nature-based tourism in an ASEAN Heritage Park; Manaf et al. (2018) which explored sustainable tourism using the example of one village in Indonesia; Poudel and Nyaupane (2017) which modelled the decision making by tourists visiting an eco-tourism destination in Annapurna Conservation Area in Nepal.

▶ REFERENCES

Abend, G. (2008). The meaning of 'theory'. Sociological Theory, 26(2), 173–199.

Al-Hammadi, F., & Sidek, H.M. (2015). An analytical framework for analysing secondary EFL writing curriculum: Approaches for writing and preparation for higher education. International Education Studies, 8(1), 59–70.

Bandyopadhyay, R., & Patil, V. (2017). 'The white woman's burden' – The racialized, gendered politics of volunteer tourism. Tourism Geographies, 19(4), 644–657.

Coolican, H. (2017). Research methods and statistics in psychology. Hove: Psychology Press.

Haddouche, H., & Salomone, C. (2018). Generation z and the tourist experience: Tourist stories and use of social networks. Journal of Tourism Futures, 4(1), 69–71.

Hammond, M. (2018) 'An interesting paper but not sufficiently theoretical': What does theorising in social research look like? Methodological Innovations, May-August, [online] https://doi.org/10.1177%2F2059799118787756.

Keith, T. (2019). Multiple regression and beyond: An introduction to multiple regression and structural equation modelling. London: Routledge.

Kim, Y., Kim, C. K, Lee, D. K., Lee, H. W, & Andrada, R. (2019). Quantifying nature-based tourism in protected areas in developing countries by using social big data. Tourism Management, 72, 249–256.

Krause, M. (2016). The meanings of theorizing. British Journal of Sociology, 67(1), 23–29.

Manaf, A., Purbasari, N., Damayanti, M., Aprilia, N., & Astuti, W. (2018). Community-based rural tourism in inter-organizational collaboration: How does it work sustainably? Lessons learned from Nglanggeran tourism village, Gunungkidul regency, Yogyakarta, Indonesia. Sustainability, 10(7), 2142.

Poudel, S., & Nyaupane, G.P. (2017). Understanding environmentally responsible behaviour of ecotourists: The reasoned action approach. Tourism Planning & Development, 14(3), 337–352.

Scott-Arthur, T., Brown, B., & Saukko, P. (2021). Conflicting experiences of health and habitus in a poor urban neighbourhood: A Bourdieusian ethnography. Sociology of Health & Illness, 43(3), 697–712.

Segovia-Pérez, M., Castro Núñez, R.B., Santero Sánchez, R., & Laguna Sánchez, P. (2020). Being a woman in An ICT job: An Analysis of the gender pay gap And discrimination in Spain. New Technology, Work and Employment, 35(1), 20–39.

Wilmot, K. (2021) Learning how to theorize in doctoral writing: A tool for teaching and learning. In C. Winberg, S. McKenna and K. Wilmot (Eds.), Building knowledge in higher education: Enhancing teaching and learning with legitimation code theory. London: Routledge.

5

The presentation of a thesis or dissertation

In the last three chapters we have looked at how you can show your understanding of your field, your application of a methodology and method, and your contribution to knowledge. In this chapter, we look at the organisation of a thesis or dissertation, drawing attention to the overall shape of the report, the constituent chapters, sections and paragraphs, and the importance of using key terms appropriately. We cover

- What is common to most reports?
- Templates for the main body of the report
- Organisation of chapters, sections, and paragraphs
- The importance of words
- Editing and proof reading
- Finding a voice
- Being critical

DOI: 10.4324/9781003161820-5

▶ WHAT IS COMMON TO MOST REPORTS?

Of course, there are many ways of writing a report but there are some things that are common to most dissertations and theses: a title, an abstract, an introduction, and a summary chapter.

Let us start with the title. Most students, and supervisors for that matter, give this little thought, it is something to be conjured up at the end. But try to think about the title from the start. It should encapsulate the big idea behind your research. Going back to online learning, something we looked at in Chapter 1, a thesis exploring student perspectives could be variously titled:

A. A survey of non-traditional students and their attitudes towards online learning.
B. Attitudes to online learning: A survey of non-traditional students.
C. Do students feel connected when learning online? A survey of non-traditional students across three courses.

There is, of course, no right or wrong choice but C works well in capturing what, we presume, is a key question (student perception of presence) for the researcher as well as the methodology used in the study. A and B are workable descriptive titles, and do mention methodology, but they do not put the aim of the research 'in lights' and do not set up reader expectations as to what follows. A good title communicates to the reader what the point of the research was.

All reports will have acknowledgements, titles, contents, perhaps a glossary, and then an abstract. As with titles, abstracts are often rattled off after everything else is done, but again why not draft out something much earlier? You can use this draft to focus on the organisation of your text, albeit it is something you will need to update as your writing gets under way. The example below shows part of a work in progress abstract for a research project in the field of online learning:

> *This is a study of MOOCs and the opportunities they provide for non-traditional learners to access education. It tells us why learners, who are not themselves already in higher*

education, sign up for these courses and what they get out of their learning experience.

The study addressed four key questions: 'What experiences did these learners have?' 'What did they see the opportunities for learning?' 'What did they see as constraints on learning?' 'What did they learn through their participation?' The study aimed to understand learners' perspectives and both surveys and interviews were carried out in order to do this.

Data were collected using questionnaires (N = 360 students) and interviews (N = 8) from a sample of learners not in higher education, who had taken one or more online courses. The study found varied experiences of participation and only a small number of learners were able to complete the full set of learning activities. Interviews uncovered the strategies used to navigate through material, the role of peer support and the value of online resources outside of the course.

The majority of learners valued their experience of learning but for personal and pedagogical reasons they were not able to cover as much of the course as they had intended. Many signed up for course that they did not complete or left at an early stage. Key reasons for non-completion was an unrealistic expectation of the time needed and gaps in background knowledge.

The study adds to the literature by presenting three types of online learning experience (committed, pragmatic, and surface). Learner characteristics are important in explaining learning experiences but so are contextual conditions including reliable access to technology, meaningful tutor intervention, and user-centred design of the learning material. Recommendations are made for learners, teachers, and institutions wishing to promote the use of eLearning.

Helpful in this draft is that is sets out:

What the study is about: 'This is a study of MOOCs and the opportunities they provide for non-traditional students to access education.'

The aim of the study: 'The research was designed to explore student experiences of MOOCs' followed by the research questions.

The methodology employed: 'This was a mixed methods study using both quantitative and qualitative methods,' with brief details to follow.

The key findings: 'The study found varied experiences of participation and only a small number of students were able to complete the full set of learning activities,' again followed by further detail.

The key contribution: The study adds to the literature by presenting three types of learning experience (committed, pragmatic, and surface) in relation to online learning.

Expectations regarding the abstract differ but 200–300 words are not unusual in a thesis, something less in a dissertation. An abstract is generally written in the third person even if your study is not. It is not usual to cite literature.

After the abstract, the first chapter in most reports is an introduction. This could be an expanded version of the abstract setting out in more detail why the research was undertaken and the context of the research. As you begin the introduction, you might launch straight into the subject of the research and the key research contribution of the study, 'This is a study of learner perspectives on their experience of learning within MOOCS....' An alternative is to lead into the key question more gently:

My interest in eLearning began when I was a teacher and I noticed the enthusiasm that students had for computers. At first I was pleased to see their interest in computing and the effect that computers had on their motivation. Over time I became less certain. I wanted to know more about what they were learning as they navigated their way through virtual worlds. This felt important as people were talking about computers uncritically, they were noticing behavioural changes and assuming important learning was taking place. I shifted from being a computer enthusiast to being a follower of others, happy to keep up with trends but not ahead of them.

This changed for me when I was introduced to MOOCs. I took a couple of online professional programmes and rated highly the access to classroom examples and the support from my peers.

It was a struggle to find the time to fully engage with the courses but I thought the experience was worth it. Even if there were shortcomings in the material, and some of it needed updating, my enthusiasm for technology seemed to be coming back. But was my positive experience of online courses shared by others? I needed to ask if I was I being sucked in again to uncritically accept technology. I needed to find out more and this was my motivation to undertake this study. I wanted to address a really straightforward question: why do learners, who are not in higher education, sign up for these courses and what do they get out of their learning experience?. The answers though were far from straightforward.

This kind of introduction works well in bringing the reader into the story of your research as well as to forewarn them of the background and experiences that may shape how you see, in this case, the use of technology. It is, indeed, increasingly common to describe the personal significance of a study in dissertations and theses but whether or not this comes first, later, or not at all, will come down to individual preference.

After you have set out the big idea underlying the research, the introduction generally sets out the key concepts and theories related to the study as well as an indication of the practical and academic areas to which you are proposing to contribute. For example, imagine as in the previous chapter my study concerns sustainable tourism then I might set out where the term originated and the meanings attached to it:

The idea of sustainable tourism captures the idea of a fairer and more environmentally friendly tourist practice. The term emerged in the latter half of the twentieth century but quickly became used by policy makers and practitioners when discussing tourism. The goal of sustainability has been promoted by the United Nations, European Union and many other international organisations. Although sustainability has an obvious focus on protecting environmental resources and conserving heritage it has been evoked to promote inter-cultural understanding and poverty alleviation as well. There are key tensions in the use of term, for example is it simply aspirational or does it have a practical value? This is explored in the literature review in Chapter 2.

The introduction generally covers the settings for the study, too. How far to go with this varies from project to project. For example, if you were reporting on a case study then the detail of the case – whether the particular school, hospital, or playground is typical or unusual, the level of cultural and physical resources available, the history of the setting, and so on – will probably be discussed later when explaining the methodology. In other, perhaps less context rich studies, you might want to provide an overview in the introduction itself. For example, if yours is an investigation into government controls on tourist development in small island states you might cover policy and practice in your introduction but put the literature review on tourist development in Chapter 2 and then report on interviews with government ministers in Chapter 3. However, there are no hard and fast rules.

The introduction will wrap up by providing a signpost to the chapters that follow. These are short summaries of what the reader will expect to find, as in the example below:

> *In Chapter 2, I look at what has been said about decision making and tourist destinations in the literature. This is presented as a narrative review drawing on academic journals, books and so-called grey literature. This review is organised around models of decision making; values and tourism; criticisms of rational choice theory; the increasing role of social media. In commenting on the literature I draw attention to a bias among researchers towards rational choice models and identify how my research addresses a theoretical gap.*

There will inevitably be a tension in the introduction between saying too little, that is, failing to prime the reader, and saying too much, repeating what is going to be covered later. Where you draw the line will be your call, but the key is not to overdo the detail; the introduction is a guide to what is coming, not the whole thing itself. This means that the introduction is generally a shorter chapter than others in your report.

Jumping to the opposite end of the report most students include a final chapter providing a reminder of what has been covered and its significance. It is easy to be cynical of the adage put out by public relations gurus: 'say what you are going to say, say it and remind your audience what you have said,' but in the case of a long academic report this is actually useful advice. This is because your text is complex and will tax the reader's attention. You will have lost sight of this complexity as you know your study inside out, but your reader will struggle and will get lost. Further, readers are unlikely to read the whole thing in one sitting, they will dip in and out. This means they will lose the thread and forget some of what you have told them. Readers really would welcome summaries throughout the report and a grand recap at the end, especially one that recalls the research questions and key findings. You should also remind the reader about the contribution of the research and develop the recommendations for stakeholders. It is increasingly common to present some kind of personal reflection on the process of carrying out the study, too.

▶ TEMPLATES FOR THE MAIN BODY OF THE REPORT

We have a title, an abstract, an introduction, and conclusions or summary chapter, but what comes in between? Undoubtedly, the template that is most promoted on research degree programmes, and in the associated literature, is the *standard format* (see Table 5.1) covering chapters on literature review, methodology findings, and discussion. These chapters are generally of roughly equal length.

The strength of the standard format is that it presents the project as unfolding in a clear, logical sequence so that is easy for the reader to follow and for the writer to work towards. It can suit a great many student research projects and can be easily adapted to include conceptual/theoretical reviews as part of the literature review or as chapters in their own right. Findings can be presented in more than one chapter, too, for example findings from interviews in one chapter, findings from secondary data analysis

TABLE 5.1 Different templates for a thesis or dissertation

Format	Likely structure	Pros and cons
The standard format	Introduction Literature review Methodology Findings/results Discussion	*Pros* • easy for the reader to follow • imposes an order onto the writer • conceptual framework/theoretical framework easily integrated *Cons* • does not capture the iterative nature of many projects
The action research – or other practice-based project	Varied but may contain: Introduction to action research methodology Identification of a problem Cycles of implementing solutions, evaluating solutions Reflection and discussion	*Pros* • captures the iterative nature of the project • focused on problem identification • allows for integration of professional and academic resources *Cons* • no agreed template • discussion of contribution to literature can be neglected
Ethnographic or in-depth case study	Varied formats but typically contains: Description of a context Literature review Chapters on the different phenomena uncovered during the research Discussion	*Pros* • allows for a focus on developing concepts and thick descriptions • flexible – no constraining template • allows for 'story-telling' or narrative writing *Cons* • no clear template to work from (may be a plus) • readers may need to hunt for the data
Inductive studies and grounded theory	Varied formats but may follow an iterative structure with literature integrated at the analysis and discussion stage	*Pros* • literature review not assumed to be first step of the study • flexible – no single constraining template *Cons* • no clear template to work from (may be a plus) • readers may get bogged down in the detailed description of the process of the research

in the next. Those following the standard format can find many models on which to base their writing and indeed the format is also used in many academic articles.

A weakness in the standard format is that it is very difficult to show changes in direction within a project. For example, how should you weave literature only uncovered at the end of a project, into a review which was ostensibly carried out at the start? Perhaps this does not really matter, the reader simply wants to know what the studies covered not when and how they were accessed. But for many students, this just does not feel right. The standard format might also need some serious re-working if the integration of data is to be properly presented in a mixed methods study or a multiple case study.

There are more flexible approaches to organising your text if you decide to take them. This is particularly important in the case of action research and other practitioner methodologies. Here accounts often begin with an introduction to a setting and a discussion of the principles behind action research before leading onto to chapters taking the reader through a cycle or cycles of planning, implementation, and evaluation. There may be a final chapter too that looks at the implications of the research and the relatability of the findings to other settings. Other explicitly inductive (or bottom-up) approaches also benefit from a more iterative structure. For example, grounded theorists engage with literature during and not before the analysis of data and they may not want to include a formal chapter on literature review at all. As with action research, grounded theorists will need to consider whether their contribution to knowledge is at a local or wider level and how they wish to report the discussion of their findings.

Perhaps the most interesting innovations in format have come in ethnography and in-depth qualitative inquiry, including case study. Here, there is special emphasis on the author as tool of data collection and there might be prominent sections in the report, or indeed a separate chapter, explaining the relationship of researcher to the context. The later part of the report, rather than offering a single 'findings' chapters, may offer a number of chapters which provide 'thick description' of key events or processes witnessed within the study. Some ethnographers are keen to provide narratives of their research as their in-depth immersion in their study context leads them to be aware of the many different versions of the events they have could have written; it would be artificial to wrap these up as 'findings.' For some, this leads to a more literary account which shows, rather than tells, the reader what took place.

Alternative formats can seem radical but at heart they are simply different ways of showing knowledge of a field, knowledge of methodology, and a contribution to field just as in any other approach. Often, however, students working with alternative formats have a different take on what such knowledge consists of and how to go about producing it. For example, in practice-based research, showing knowledge of your field may lead into a threading of both personal and professional experiences in a report and making a contribution will cover both local ('Does this innovation help me be a better practitioner?') and academic ('Are there general principles others can learn from here?') implications.

Templates provide a tool for the writing up of your project and you need such a tool to keep your story on track. However, templates can feel restrictive and if you find yourself with one that does not give you the flexibility you need, then you need to innovate. At times a small change in terminology, for example, substituting *what others have said*, for *literature review*, can lead you to think about the nature of academic knowledge in a more creative way. Even substitution of the word *findings* for *results*, or vice versa, can open up a different way of reporting your analysis of data. There is no need to throw out existing templates, or templates you have been recommended, but you do need to think about why and to what degree they suit your study. If you want to take a novel approach then explain to your supervisor why this is; it is always a good idea to find, and critically review, a thesis following a similar format to the one you are proposing and you do need to have, or help find, an external examiner who is flexible and indeed welcoming of novelty.

▶ ORGANISATION OF CHAPTERS, SECTIONS, AND PARAGRAPHS

Each chapter usually begins with a signpost or listing of what is going to be covered, this is followed by the sections themselves until the final paragraph wraps up the paragraph or leads into the next section. The example below shows a 'bare bones' approach to signposting, in this case a guide to what is coming in a review of literature on riots. This works perfectly well to orient the reader, but make sure the bullet headers exactly match those of the succeeding sections; paraphrasing will confuse:

This chapter is divided into five sections which cover

- accessing the literature
- the concept of a riot
- the reasons for rioting
- the attribution of riots
- the perceived consequences of riots
- implications for the study

In contrast, if you wanted to remind the reader as to how the story of the research is unfolding you might go for a more narrative approach as below:

> In the previous chapter, I set the scene. I explained my interest in the topic and how riots have been perceived differently not just depending on personality, for example aversion or not to risk taking, but one's position in society. We saw the practical and theoretical importance of understanding different perceptions of riots and of noticing the vocabulary used to describe rioting.

> The project thus became organised around one overarching question, 'Why do people riot?' This is not by any means a new question and in this chapter I look at what others have written. The chapter begins by explaining how I accessed the literature and this also covers a discussion of how I organised my reading of the literature. The main sections then cover the keys findings

from the literature. There are organised around the themes of: the concept of a riot; the reasons for rioting; the attribution of riots; the perceived consequences of riots. *I reflect on what I learnt from the literature and its significance for my study in a final section:* implications for my study.

This kind of approach can better engage your readers, but they will be irritated if you overdo the contextualisation and do not get on with the chapter itself.

When it comes to the content of a chapter, it is really helpful for the reader to see clearly labelled sections and sub-sections. These sections can be numbered, but they do not need to be if you use consistent formats for title headers and sub headers. If you do go with numbers avoid too many levels, for example a section that is labelled 2.3.3.2 is going to confuse rather than help.

Each section within a chapter may have its own signposting and a summary or reflection at its close. As an example, those studying community often cite, McMillan and Chavis's (1986) definition of community, a typical exposition of which is given below. This section begins with a signpost in a short first paragraph. This is followed by four main paragraphs, only the one on membership is given here, and a brief final reflection paragraph to close the description:

> *There are four elements that help define sense of community according to early work by McMillan and Chavis (1986). These are membership; influence; reinforcement; and shared emotional connection.*
>
> *Firstly, membership. This concerns a 'feeling of belonging, of being a part.' These feelings provide the sense of safety and trust which allows for the expression of emotions. The key thing about membership is that it creates boundaries: there are those that belong and those who do not. Boundaries are double-edged – you cannot have a community without boundaries, but boundaries can also be restrictive and can involve pain and rejection to those who do not belong. In discussing membership, McMillan and Chavis cover the importance of*

emotional safety, personal investment, and the need for a common symbol system.

(...)

Of course, there are many other ways to look at community and the ideas of membership and boundaries is taken up most notably in work on community of practice. I have dwelt on Chavis and McMillan as they sum up many of the ideas which are core to sense of community literature. However, one key question remains: how far can concepts of developed in physical communities work in the highly connected online communities that exist today?

There is no strict rule about chapter length, but if one chapter turns out much longer than the others, then think about breaking it up. For example, a long findings chapter on perspectives of community can be broken into a chapter on respondents' view of their locality and another on attitudes to incomers. In some mixed methods study, findings may be presented in different chapters according to method, say, interview data, and then survey data. However, it is often more elegant to integrate findings right away if that is a possibility. In similar vein, if you have a very long section within a chapter then think about how you can break this up. Long sections usually arise because you have thrown too many ideas together and it should not be too difficult to spot how to split it. In contrast, if you have a very short section this can usually be merged with another.

Within a section, paragraph length will vary but four to nine sentences around a single idea is often recommended. Paragraphs should not be overlong or bring in more than one idea. Wherever natural, keep sentence length to one or two lines and try to limit the use of brackets and subordinate clauses at the start of the sentence unless you think it works and/or you cannot see a way round this. It is, for example, difficult to follow the sentence:

Given the previous comments of interviewees concerning policing, and given their specific complaints about an earlier incident of wrongful arrest, it was unexpected that many respondents appeared to want a greater police presence in their community.

This can be rewritten as two sentences:

> *It was unexpected that many interviewees appeared to want a greater police presence in their community given their concerns about community relationships. These concerns were enhanced by a recent case of wrongful arrest.*

You may, further, think about the variety of sentence length you are offering your reader. For example, try experimenting with some shorter sentence when your text is becoming very dense.

▶ THE IMPORTANCE OF WORDS

Entry into, and feeling part of, an academic community involves understanding academic vocabulary and using it with discrimination. Academics tend to use words that are more formal, ones that are not part of everyday speech. They bring in specialist terms in respect to methodology (such as constructivism, phenomenology) and concepts (such as neoliberalism, functionalism, socialisation) and when they use more everyday terms (such as community, learning, role play) they do so in ways which differ, sometimes quite subtly, from familiar usage.

When it comes to verbs, academics might write about interviewees *articulating* an idea or an idea being *contested* within the literature. It is important to appreciate the nuances. *Articulating* might be just the right word if you want to imply there was a working through of an idea not just the simple communication of something already formed. Articulation, then is not quite the same as *said* or *explained*, still less *admitted, argued, explicated,* or *proposed*. When we say something is *contested* in the literature, it implies there was an argument about principles, something more at stake than simply A *disagreed with* B. Be sure that you use the word that conveys your meaning precisely.

Then, there are technical terms which define procedures and processes in ways that everyday language does not. Thus *interviews*, not conversations, may have been carried out, interview *schedules*, rather than list of questions, were created and these schedules may have been *semi-structured*. In presenting findings, we should not confuse *data, information,* or *evidence*. The data are raw, information is the data made meaningful and the evidence is how information has been organised to support a conclusion. When it comes to surveys then we might differentiate *questionnaire survey* from say *observation survey*, and we should be precise as to whether the questionnaire has *items* or *questions*.

In coding of qualitative data, terms are not so consistently used. This means it is important to define what *codes, categories, concepts,* and *themes* mean if used in your study and then apply these terms consistently. In writing about data collection, it is usual to use *respondents* for those who completed your questionnaire and *interviewees* for those you interviewed. *Participants* can be used for interviewees but may imply something more, perhaps a level of co-participation in the research. Be thoughtful when using terms to describe the roles of the people you have been researching. For example, you may be researching *students* when concerned with participants' learning, but *children* when looking at family life, and *young people* when considering peer groups and leisure.

As a general point be as consistent as far possible in all you do. In some cultures, it is considered good style to vary vocabulary, but this is less usual in writing academic texts, particularly in writing aimed at international audiences. A little variety is fine, after all it can be tedious to read what the interviewees *said* for the umpteenth time, but do not search the dictionary to find 'posh' alternatives such as *explicated, elucidated,* or *expounded*, you will almost certainly use them inappropriately. If an idea can be conveyed perfectly well in everyday speech, then go for it; it is clearer if you write about 'fitting in' an interview rather than 'accommodating the time demands of an interviewee.'

Throughout your writing, try to ensure you vocabulary is consistent with your ontological/epistemological stance. If you share at least some positivist assumptions then you will be writing about what happened to the people involved; if you take an interpretivist stance you will be focusing more on what people did, and the meanings they put on events. The vocabulary you use will reflect your stance. Interpretivists use terms such as *agency, meaning making, findings,* and *consequences,* and positivists terms such as *behaviour, behavioural triggers, results,* and *outcomes.* If you share aspects of both stances, then be clear as to when you are writing about agency and when about causal conditions. Think carefully about whether you want to say X *caused Y, X shaped Y, X led to Y, Y* was *possibly a result* of X. Language is important. Using the appropriate terms helps the story hang together.

The use of the first person

It is increasingly common in social research reporting to use the first person and the least problematic use of this is when you are explaining the steps that have been taken. Of course, you could put your whole account in the passive and write, for example, that 'a questionnaire survey *was distributed* to a pilot group of potential participants. Six *were returned.* The questionnaire *was amended* (question 7 and 8 *were reworded*) and *was then delivered* to the main study group.' This is not wrong but, to me at least, it appears convoluted. It also introduces an ambiguity; the questionnaire *was distributed/was amended/questions were reworded* but by whom? To address any doubt, you could put *was distributed by the researcher* but this feels clumsy, why not '*I distributed* the questionnaires?'

You could, then, extend the use of the first person when directing the reader through a report and rather than have '*this chapter is organised into five chapters*' put '*I have organised this chapter around five sections.*' Arguably this signals a clearer ownership of the text, but the gain is marginal. When saying *this chapter is organised into five sections* there is no ambiguity; the reader knows it is you who has organised the report as your name is on it and you wrote it.

The first-person plural is also used in writing to signal a community, for example 'as human beings living in complicated societies, *we* should be aware of the need to compromise if we are to live together harmoniously.' *We* is a useful shorthand here and it would feel odd to write of human beings as if researchers and the readers were not themselves members of the human race! Some might object that the use of *we* is being overly rhetorical – the reader can become sucked into a way of thinking rather than reminded to keep a critical distance – but this is going too far. The use of we, can, however, become problematic when it refers, almost as a kind of sleight of hand, to a particular experience, or standpoint. 'We' would probably object if we read 'as human beings living in complicated societies, we should be aware of the need to dominate others.' As in all things then context is important.

Die-hard resistance to the more extensive use of the first person comes from those who see social research as an objective discipline, one that should follow the standards set in natural science. A scientist would not say *I heated the compound*, but the *compound was heated*, because it does not matter who applied the heat, the same phenomenon would be observed. In the same way, social researchers should not say *I distributed the questionnaire* as it does not matter who did the distributing. Underlying this belief is that anyone addressing the same questions, following the same procedures should reach the same conclusions. Of course, it is not possible to prove replication in social science as we can never research exactly the same context twice, but the use of the passive is a reminder that we should strive for objectivity and not let our individuality express itself on the page. This is contested by others, who argue it matters a great deal who did the research as each researcher will ask different questions and collect and interpret data in their own way. Thus, behind the rather trivial question as to whether you can use the first person or not lie some far from trivial questions as to whether social research should present itself as a science or not.

▶ EDITING AND PROOF READING

After a period of drafting and redrafting, there comes a point when you have got the main story on the page and it is time to tidy it up. Please do not just give it a quick look over and submit it.

To pick up the points made about the process of writing in Chapter 1, there is the intensive work of revising, editing, and proof reading.

Think of *revising* as being prepared to make significant changes to the structure of the text. Look once again at the overall flow, the arguments you are putting forward, and the evidence for your claims. Is it all there? Check once again that the sections are placed in a logical order, that the signposting works, and the summaries are concise and complete. Check the research questions are explicitly answered, the contribution explained, and that the recommendations for different stakeholders are set out. Look for omission and repetitions – it is not unusual for chunks to have gone missing or duplicated in the cutting and pasting of text during the drafting process.

In revising, it is easy to focus on the parts of the text that hang together and quickly scan the odd paragraphs and sections that do not. The analogy here is with the amateur musician who carefully rehearses all the parts of a score that they can play but glosses over the parts with which they have difficulty in the hope it will be all right on the night. Like this musician, you have to focus on the parts that are causing difficulty and some 90 percent of your attention may be taken up with the 10 percent which is problematic.

Next, the *editing* stage. Think of this as a half-way between revising and proof reading. At this stage, you are happy with the organisation of the text but now pay closer attention to sentence construction and the links between sentences and paragraphs. Look at the vocabulary – are you using terms not only consistently but in ways that reflect your epistemological stance? In terms of sentence construction, look for overlong or clumsy sentences and unnecessary repetition. You will be surprised at how often you have redundancy or tautology in a sentence for example 'writing is difficult because there are so many difficulties associated with the art of writing.' Pay attention to connectors (words such as *besides, in addition, furthermore, however, nevertheless*), do they capture the exact association between sentences you want to convey? Look out for ideas that should come in twos but have come adrift. If you have *on the one hand* you should later have *on the other hand*; if you have *not only* this is usually followed later by *but also*.

Finally, *proof reading*. The closer you are to the text the more you will be reading for meaning, not paying attention to form, so leave as much time as feasible between completing the draft and the final step of proofreading. When proofreading you need to try to see the text through the eyes of a reader, tell yourself that the text no longer belongs to you. It might help to do this if you try proof reading pages out of order to distract your attention from the story. If you think proof reading is a chore, and the reader really should not be bothered about a clumsy sentence or an apostrophe in the wrong place, then think again. Readers will become irritated by your errors and examiners will be asking 'Why should I trust you as an honest reporter of this project when you care so little for my experience of being a reader?'

There is much popular debate about how far language rules should be followed but most linguists are clear that rules should be descriptive (i.e. in line with convention) rather than prescriptive (rules which should be obeyed even if they have become out of date). Conventions are really important as it is very disruptive for the reader when they are broken. For example, there is a convention that contractions (won't, it's, can't, and so on) are avoided in academic writing. There is no logical reason why this is the case but fluent reading rests on prediction, you must see what you expect to see. When faced with a *won't, it's,* or *can't* the reader will stop and think, 'Something is wrong here, what is it? Oh yes, they have they used a contraction.' In other words, the reader is forced to think about how you are organising your writing, rather than the content, and that is doing your reader a great disservice. Of course, conventions do, slowly, change but let others push for them. It was, for example, once considered bad style to split infinitives (*to boldly go* rather than *to go boldly*), but few today would give this a second look. The use of 'I' in academic writing was, as we have seen, once considered off limits but is quite acceptable in most fields today. It was once thought bad style to start a sentence with *and* or *but*. Now it is not unusual, even if you should do so sparingly.

Almost always the time and attention needed for proof reading is under-estimated. Proof reading is much better done in stages rather than all at once.

First, you could work on citations ('Is there a consistent pattern for the use of brackets and page referencing?' 'Is there a date or alphabetical for strings of references?') and references ('Are they all there?' 'Are they formatted consistently?' 'How have online sources been referenced?').

Next, look for line breaks, for tables that span across two or more pages, and the application of styles for *Captions, Headers, Normal Text,* and *Quotes.* Are you using lower and upper case consistently for proper names – is it the race equalities act or the Race Equalities Act, is it Marxism or marxism, Australian or australian? Are you mixing "double" and 'single' inverted commas? When it comes to numbers is it ten or 10? Do not let anything go. You will miss many typos, we all do, but do not add to the list by ignoring the things you can put right.

Finally, use spell checks as these will pick up typos, repeated words, double-spacing between words and so on. Using the variant of spell checker that you have been recommended (Is it summarise or summarize, programme or program, practice and advice as noun or verb?) go through each suggestion manually, avoid the *Change All* option no matter how appealing. Do not over rely on spell checkers as they will not pick up on errors such as *researches show* when you mean *researchers show.* Tick the box which says *Grammar Check,* or use a dedicated online grammar checker, and start another check. This can be helpful for noticing inconsistencies, say between plural subject and singular verb form, but do not accept stylistic suggestions without a great deal of thought. Grammar checkers do not know the readers for whom you are writing and their expectations of your text.

If using English as a second language the process of revising, editing, and proof reading is almost bound to take a lot longer. In addition to the earlier advice look out for 'false friends,' words that do not quite have the same meaning in English as in your first language. For example, the word *actually* is used, but used sparingly, to draw attention to what has *in fact* happened, often for emphasis. It is fine in the sentence 'In spite of their earlier reservations, the tourists had *actually* enjoyed visiting the national park.' In some European languages actually suggests *happening now*, in the present, something quite different.

Pay particular attention to connectors. For example, many students with ESL mix up on the *contrary/in contrast/contrariwise*. *On the contrary* is a direct countervailing point or argument, as in 'Ministers thought the new policy was helpful, but *on the contrary*, it simply created confusion.' *In contrast* is used for pointing out inconsistency but this need not be in direct opposition to a previous statement or finding. For example, 'the teachers were overwhelmingly enthusiastic about the changes, *in contrast* pupils had reservations.' In most cases, you want *in contrast* not *on the contrary*. *Contrariwise* means in the opposite way – for example a handle turned in an anticlockwise direction – and it is unlikely that you will use it. Try to avoid *also* as a way of linking two sentences, it seems lazy, almost as if you do not know how to connect two ideas.

Finding the exact word is difficult and you may not be aware of subtle differences. For example, *therefore* and *thus* can sometimes be used interchangeably but *therefore* feels more of an inescapable conclusion, *thus* is better when introducing the background that makes an action explicable. The sentence 'they felt alienated, therefore they were open to taking part in the protests' feels wrong as the connection between alienation and protest is by no means a necessary one – if there was such a strong connection they were would be some kind of protest every day. 'They felt alienated, thus they were open to taking part in the protest' works better as it suggests that protesting was not the only possible consequence of their alienation.

Second language learners, and not just second language learners, often have difficulty with tenses. Unless you have strong reasons for doing something different, your report is written in the past tense, it explains what you *did* and what you *found out.* For example, 'the aim of the questionnaire survey *was* to gather data on the attitudes to policy and whether respondents *were* receptive to the proposed changes.' In the same vein get reported speech right. For example, it is fine in a study of holiday destinations to quote Interviewee A as replying, 'I want to visit somewhere which is different, it has to have a special vibe.' However, in reported speech this becomes, 'Interviewee A said that he *wanted* to go somewhere which *was* different, it *had to* have a different vibe.' When referring to the literature as a whole you might use the present tense or present perfect if you are stressing that the issues remain live at the time of writing, for example, riots *have been studied* comprehensively over the last twenty years and policing *has been reported/is reported* as a key issue. However, if you are describing a particular book or article published in the past then check that you have used the simple past tense as in, 'X (2001) *studied* police behaviour and *found* this *had* a strong impact on the community response.' On the subject of time, remember too that your reader may be reading your report in one, five, ten or more years from now. Use phrases such as *at the time of writing* rather than *now,* or *at the present time.*

It is a really open question as to how much consideration you should be given if you are a user of English as a second language. It takes many hours of study to appreciate the nuances of a language. Academic journals are becoming increasingly conscious that the use of English as an international language is distorting their output and really is not fair; prospective contributors are being judged not on what they have to say but how they say it. Reviewers will try to show flexibility and journal editors may be able to provide language support. Something similar is happening with dissertations and theses. Most examiners are tolerant of errors and inconsistencies in ways they were not before and most institutions will offer support. Students may, if they can afford it, seek out professional proof-readers, albeit there are limits on how much help they can give. However, this should not detract from the fact that it is your responsibility to get your text as clear as possible. The sticking point for many examiners is when they have to guess your intended meaning. You really need to find a first language user to look at your text before submitting it. Having English as a second language may not be such a disadvantage when it comes to writing as it forces you into the position of being intensely curious about words and structures which native speakers may take for granted. You may end up more knowledgeable and more alive to language use than native speakers.

▶ FINDING A VOICE

Finding a voice is about your identity as a writer. It is expressed in the decisions you make on which problems you think are worth researching and how you go about investigating these problems. However, it is also conveyed in the way you write – the vocabulary you use, your use, or not, of the first person, your sentence construction, the degree to which you are willing to assert a position. When it comes to writer voice, there is an increasing emphasis, at least in the teaching of writing, on a standard academic voice and we start by looking at what this looks like. However, there are alternatives and we look at some of these, drawing on examples from academic journals.

The standard voice

Just as many students are led into using a standard format for organising their text, they are often expected to write using a standard academic voice. This is the voice of an objective and rather pedantic reporter. You are someone who shows attention to detail when it comes to describing and interpreting data, you are careful in the claims you make, and overall you are exacting, modest, and principled. Your writing aims to be as value free as possible, you avoid rhetoric, and you are restrained when it comes to the use of the first person. You aim to provide clarity and coherence through your structuring of sections and your use of signposting, tables, and summaries. The claims you make are carefully supported and your interpretations are hedged, you recognise that you are offering a contribution and other conclusions are possible. Here, Segovia-Pérez et al. (2020:21) are writing about a gender pay gap in Spain. The paper begins:

> *The gender wage gap is a well-known phenomenon. Numerous studies and organisations have confirmed that women are paid less than men (UN Women, 2015). This is partly due to segregation and gender stereotypes; women are linked to traditionally 'female' occupations, and these are associated with inferior working conditions and lower pay. (Prokos et al., 2009; Stockdale and Nadler, 2013)*

The argument is put (a *gender wage gap exists*), the evidence is provided that *women are paid less than men*, and rather than seeing such a gap as an accident or random occurrence, it is argued that it is something that can be explained by segregation and gender stereotypes. The tone is measured, *there is a pay-gap* not *there is a quite unacceptable/intolerable/unsupportable pay-gap* and there *have been numerous studies showing this*, rather than a *mass*, *plethora*, or *raft* of studies. At the end of the paper, after presentation and interpretation of new data, a conclusion is reached:

> *In conclusion, our findings reflect the ways in which gender stereotypes affect women, who are professionally penalised, who are segregated to some occupations, and whose progression is hampered. Moreover, the obtained results stress the relevance of a sector approach for addressing the challenges that the ICT profession faces in terms of gender equality. While in ICT-intensive sectors, a cultural change is needed to fight the effects of a male dominated environment, in non-ICT-intensive sectors, a crucial factor would be the implementation of human resources policies that break with the current gendered organisational management policies in order to tackle sticky floor problems. Resolving gender disparities in the ICT professions still has a long way to go, but in a globalised high-tech world where labor markets are increasingly interconnected, it is necessary to gather information from different cultural contexts, in order to design effective policies. Studies such as that presented in this paper may contribute to a better diagnosis, and lead to possible strategies and solutions. (Segovia-Pérez et al., 2020:36)*

Again, the tone is measured. The passive is used (*a cultural change is needed*, not *we need to contribute to a cultural change*) to distance the reader from the text and recommendations are hypothetical (*a crucial factor would be the implementation of human resources policies*, not *we need new policies*). The authors know that studies such as theirs do not change the world or turn the way we think about the world upside down, but they may contribute to a better diagnosis of a problem. Paradoxically perhaps, expressing a case cautiously can make an argument more persuasive as you, the author, are not asking the reader to cross an emotional barrier to engage with the text; the Segovia-Pérez et al. paper can easily attract more than a self-identified feminist audience.

The standard voice is used for both empirical and more theoretical reporting. Here, Scott-Arthur et al. (2021) are discussing community health and they show their concern for a theoretical understanding from the off:

> *An extensive literature suggests that people of low socioeconomic status suffer more from ill health and have a lower life expectancy than affluent groups; these inequalities have also become wider in the UK in the last decade due to austerity politics (Marmot et al., 2020). Factors contributing to poor health in deprived neighbourhoods include lack of access to healthy food (Donkin et al. 1999; Morland et al., 2002; Stafford et al., 2007), crime and lack of safety leading to limited mobility (Saelens et al., 2003, Suminski et al., 2005, Burgoyne et al., 2008), poor services and infrastructures (Cattell et al., 2008) and stress and hopelessness fuelling mental health problems and substance misuse (Cummins et al., 2007). However, it has been observed that social belonging and networks and a sense of pride in the community promote health and wellbeing. (Smith & Anderson, 2018)*

> *In this paper, we will interrogate these observations by using a Bourdieusian conceptual framework (Bourdieu, 1979, 1990). Bourdieu is frequently used in medical sociology to highlight how poor people's lifestyle is constrained by their habitus (e.g. Abel & Frolich, 2012; Hoeeg et al., 2020; Oncini, 2020; Williams, 1995). The article discusses how patterns of habitus and distinctions in poor neighbourhoods complicate notions of*

healthy behaviours or lifestyles and also shine new conceptual light on the enabling, constraining and differentiating nature of habitus in relation to health.

The voice is similar as in Segovia-Pérez et al. The authors are reporting matter-of-factly on social issues, not making a rhetorical or emotion packed argument. Their claim is that people of low socioeconomic status suffer more from ill health and have a lower life expectancy than affluent groups and they cite an extensive literature to support this. The reasons for these lower health outcomes are presented, again citing evidence in the form of other studies, and a conclusion reached that 'patterns of habitus and distinctions can shine new conceptual light on the enabling, constraining and differentiating nature of habitus in relation to health.' In fact, there is jump from citing the empirical evidence to saying why Bourdieu's theory may offer particular insight into the problem and we would need to read further into the paper to appreciate why this jump was made.

The earlier Segovia-Pérez et al. paper was much more of an empirical report and Scott-Arthur et al. are much more focused on making a contribution to theory and how far Bourdieu's ideas might explain a particular problem. However, both papers strike an impersonal and objective tone and, at its best, this kind of academic writing treats the reader with respect. Researchers are not seeking to convince by rhetoric but by evidence. At times the standard voice can feel quite bland but it does not need to be. Segovia-Pérez et al. begin, *The gender wage gap is a well-known phenomenon* and Scott-Arthur et al. (2021) start by saying that *an extensive literature suggests that people of low socioeconomic status suffer more from ill health and have a lower life expectancy.* These are both direct and arresting statements.

The reflective voice

It is common in reporting professional inquiry, and in many qualitative research studies as well, to strike a more reflective and personal tone. The rationale for the reflective voice is a belief that what we research (what questions are worth asking, what methods are most suitable) and the judgments we make (how we read the literature, how we interpret the data) is not value free. It matters a great deal who is conducting the research, for if two researchers started investigating the same question they would probably come up with different answers. Reflection is, further, core to many forms of professional development and is a natural stance to take when conducting research into practice. There may be aesthetic reasons, too, for submitting a personalised account as the reader is likely to be more engaged if there is a good story line to follow. In the extract below Davis (2021:39) discusses the role of reflexivity in her research on how participants dealt with myocardial infarction (or 'heart attacks') and quotes some of her own thesis to illustrate, in this case, the role of insider knowledge when interviewing people from a shared South Asian background:

Interview was used as a means of data collection. Commonality between the researcher and the researched enabled an easy familiarity and facilitated rapport, thereby yielding rich data. In this account of my first interview, I highlight how being of South Asian origin, and privileging an 'inside knowledge,' allowed me to feel part of the milieu, trading stories of the part of India we are from:

"I knock on the door and wait patiently. I am wearing a contemporary styled cotton 'salwar' and I check the dupatta is properly draped across the shoulders. The door opens ... I smile and say 'hello'... with a beaming smile the gentleman leads me to the lounge .... I remove my shoes, walk across as a lady enters, wiping her hands on her dupatta, and she embraces me and calls beti, we sit down and then the lady asks "chai?" I say "no thank you...". "Coffee?" I refuse (as it was Ramadan fasting time for them)... and I wait and we sit and smile at each other ... and I begin ......". (Davis, 2018:100)

My presence was felt like a researcher, asking questions and probing, however on the other hand, I was a South Asian, one of them. At first, I reflected that the similarity in ethnic identity created this sense of belonging, building the spontaneous relationship – with the participants I was interviewing (Davis, 2018). Nevertheless, upon further pondering, I had to acknowledge that perhaps the participants may find it easier to work with researchers from other ethnic backgrounds, as the 'insider knowledge' is like a double-edged sword.

(...)

Therefore, I concluded that no matter who is conducting research on whom, researchers do probe into other's lives to explore the phenomena. Consequently, the qualities of a good interviewer, for example listening, being sensitive and compassionate to the information shared, may help to form the building block of any relationship; these in turn would demand honesty, reciprocity, and trust – integral to data collection. Undeniably, as a nurse I may have subsumed these qualities and attributes in my clinical practice as required by my profession. Therefore, I believe it would be wise to privilege these qualities in the interviewing above any other forms of ethnic matching.

In this passage, Davis is discussing reflexivity itself. Reflexivity is not so much reflecting on the carrying out of the research but reflecting on the kind of person you are when carrying it out. In the passage Davis suggests that her research practice was shaped by her identity and by her professional values, those of 'listening, being sensitive and compassionate' which feature so heavily in nursing. Here, she shows that she understands her privileged access to her interviewees due to their shared background. However, she also notices that this privilege could also serve as constraint if interviewees are reluctant to share information which could harm such an 'easily formed relationship.' The reflective voice works well when explaining personal development during a project and seems particularly appropriate to research which draws on practice.

Those critiquing the reflexive voice largely do because they want to highlight the impersonal nature of the research process, arguing it should be, or at least it should feel, as value free as possible. A second, more practical, criticism is that reflective research can end up too chatty, self-indulgent, almost narcissist. This is avoided if the writer keeps in mind the purpose of reflection. For example, Davis is reporting what she is was wearing and what she was offered to drink as it explained something about her insider status. In other contexts, this may seem quite unnecessary. What you reveal then depends on its relevance. For example, it would irritate the reader if, in the course of reflecting on my literature review, I explained that 'I had intended to look at a particular book one day, but I overslept and then when I went in I found that I had forgotten my library card and went home. But the bus was late and then a friend called around, we went out, and would you believe it, before I knew it the whole day had gone without me doing any work.' However, the same story might be of some relevance if my study was exploring procrastination and if I had used this experience to reflect on the ways in which procrastination can seem involuntary to the procrastinator, even when it does not appear so to an observer.

The storyteller

A variation on the reflective voice is that of the storyteller. In fact, many guides to social research use the metaphor of the journey when giving advice or describing the research process. It is possible to take this metaphor literally by using some of the novelist's devices, such as the concern for descriptive detail, the development of plot lines and the showing rather than telling of events, in academic writing. Some may go further and present 'fictional' or semi-fictionalised versions of their research on the basis that all you can ever do is to tell stories about a context and you should not try to wrap things up in a sequence of events and outcomes; life is simply not like that.

Storytellers are often influenced by the idea of thick description. This was something developed by Geertz (1972) and his account of cock fighting in Bali is often cited as an example of the approach. Geertz is describing something which was probably not familiar to his readers (cock fighting) and explains the rituals, the rules, the political context, and even the language used by participants. It is, written in the first person and as readers we can understand

Geertz's position in the research context, though we do not get to see what he really felt about cock fighting itself.

> ... the fights are usually held in a secluded corner of a village in semisecrecy, a fact which tends to slow the action a little – not very much, but the Balinese do not care to have it slowed at all. In this case, however, perhaps because they were raising money for a school that the government was unable to give them, perhaps because raids had been few recently, perhaps, as I gathered from subsequent discussion, there was a notion that the necessary bribes had been paid, they thought they could take a chance on the central square and draw a larger and more enthusiastic crowd without attracting the attention of the law.
>
> They were wrong. In the midst of the third match, with hundreds of people, including, still transparent, myself and my wife, fused into a single body around the ring, a superorganism in the literal sense, a truck full of policemen armed with machine guns roared up. Amid great screeching cries of "pulisi! pulisi!" from the crowd, the policemen jumped out, and, springing into the center of the ring, began to swing their guns around like gangsters in a motion picture, though not going so far as actually to fire them. The superorganism came instantly apart as its components scattered in all directions. People raced down the road, disappeared head first over walls, scrambled under platforms, folded themselves behind wicker screens, scuttled up coconut trees. Cocks armed with steel spurs sharp enough to cut off a finger or run a hole through a foot were running wildly around. Everything was dust and panic.
>
> On the established anthropological principle, When in Rome, my wife and I decided, only slightly less instantaneously than everyone else, that the thing to do was run too. We ran down the main village street, northward, away from where we were living, for we were on that side of the ring. (Geertz, 1972:2–3)

One attractive feature of this kind of writing is that it wants you to keep reading – not something to be undervalued when it comes to academic literature. Geertz wears his scholarship lightly but this is not fiction, everything Geertz writes can be supported by evidence. For example, *cockfights go on happening, and with extraordinary frequency* relies on observation data collected over time. '*The necessary bribes*' had probably been paid was suggested by an informant, and Geertz himself was on hand to note that *people raced in all directions once the police arrived* – today the evidence could have been collected on a camera phone. The idea that the crowd was '*fused into a single body*' is much more impressionistic, though no doubt there was evidence to be collected here about the attention and joint enthusiasm shown during the fight. We are reminded, too, of Geertz's relationship to others, '*When in Rome, my wife and I decided, only slightly less instantaneously than everyone else, that the thing to do was run too,*' but we only really get to know the narrator as the researcher, a novelist might tell us how the researcher fell in love with his wife, but this would not work here!

Ethnographic accounts from the past are now routinely critiqued for accepting uncritically the status of researchers from the global north investigating the global south, but this is a different argument. The narrative style of Geertz's reporting remains attractive; many of us are drawn into these stories, and we are forewarned that we are seeing events through a particular stance of position and we cannot pretend there is an objective story to tell.

The practitioner researcher

The voice here is one that stresses the importance of addressing practical problems. Rather than begin with a theoretical position the author typically sets out a problem about a particular practice and addressing this problem informs the rest of the report. This means that, rather than carry out a general literature review, the literature is purposively searched for ideas that suggest solutions to the problem. Moreover, researchers stress that they are dealing with local rather than general problems, albeit how they address these problems may inform practice in other contexts. The approach is exemplified in this abstract of an account of cook stoves (López-Martínez and Cuanalo de la Cerda, 2020:490):

> *Different initiatives have promoted the use of improved cook stoves around the world. Their goal has been to eradicate cooking over open flame inside dwellings because it is associated with health problems, inefficient resource use and greenhouse gas emissions. Most of these improved cook stoves initiatives depend heavily on expert-generated solutions, treating users as mere recipients. However, they have had little success in terms of adoption*

rates. Their failures are due to myriad factors, highlighting the complexity of this problem. In the rural community of Yaxcabá, Mexico, most households use wood as a cooking fuel in small fire pits. As an alternative approach to this problem, we proposed a project to create an improved cook stove based on dialogue with community members. We used a systems approach to analyze the large number of variables involved in the problem. Following participatory action research approach, we worked with 17 participants forming two groups in a process of self-diagnosis, design, construction and evaluation of two improved cook stoves models. The participants stated that the resulting improved cook stoves offered multiple advantages over previous devices, particularly in sociocultural, environmental and comfort aspect.

The nature of the problem is articulated, open flame cooking is 'associated with health problems, inefficient resource use and greenhouse gas emissions.' Some alternatives to open flame cooking are referenced, or at least it is mentioned that there are different possible solutions, but the key problem is not seen as one of technology but of adoption. That is why a participatory action-oriented project was used – change needs to be carried out bottom-up, with and by those that are most affected by the problem or it will not happen at all.

The first person is used to describe actions, the authors are not passive observers. Their statement of the problem is measured not rhetorical and they do not make grandiose claims for their project. In fact, a criticism made of practice accounts is that they can be so focused on the local problem that is not always clear why they are written for a general audience in the first place. Here, the authors' intention is to provide a relatable account which others can learn from in seeking solutions to their own problems.

The counter cultural voice

Here, the voice is more strident than in our previous examples. In fact, there are many reasons to kick against the complacency of mainstream research and the way that problems are identified or researched. You might, for example, want to critique the make-up of the research community; the exclusion of researchers whose first language is not English; the division of research fields into tight disciplinary boundaries. There are also methodological criticisms to be made in most disciplines in that certain methods are favoured, be they quantitative or qualitative, and there is, some will claim, an overarching bias towards explanation over complexity.

Some of the most sustained criticisms from mainstream research have come from feminist methodologists and now from decolonising methodology. Bandyopadhyay and Patil (2017:648) capture both stances in a counter-cultural blast again volunteer tourism (this is the phenomenon of young people from the global north who work as volunteers on third sector projects in the global south). They argue for a more critical approach:

While the majority of volunteer tourism studies have acknowledged the significance of volunteer tourism and challenged conventional understandings of socio-economic change in the global South, the ways in which ideas about race and racialized gender shape volunteer tourism and development discourses are rarely spoken about. It is increasingly recognized now that development is about power – its operations, its geographies (McEwan, 2001) and indeed, development today is understood as a radical and intrusive white endeavour (Biccum, 2011; Duffield, 2005). Feminist scholars in particular have underscored the gendered and sexualized dimensions of this racialized endeavour (see for example, Alexander, 1996; Wangari, 2002). However, the overall impact of anti-racist contributions by tourism scholars to expose and challenge the racism embedded in 'whiteness' remains marginal in tourism studies. From a postcolonial feminist view, Frye (1992) describes whiteness as an assumption on the part of many Northern white women that they have the knowledge and the obligation to help women in the global South (no need to know whether they want the help or not). Kothari (2006, p. 2) asks, 'perhaps within a discourse framed around humanitarianism, cooperation and aid, raising "race" is too distracting, disruptive and demanding? Or does the silence of "race" conceal the complicity of development with racialized projects?' This paper identifies the need for further exploration of the subtle manifestations of gendered racism within volunteer tourism and insists that gender and race deserve serious discussion in volunteer tourism research. In particular, this study focuses on the history and legacies of the 'white savior complex' as it informs volunteer tourism. Contrasting the masculinism of racialized colonial processes (their feminist variants notwithstanding) with the contemporary feminization of such racialization within volunteer tourism, it also considers continuities and shifts within such processes.

Here the paper begins by identifying a gap – 'ideas about race and racialised gender are rarely spoken of.' Yet the authors are not alone in noticing this gap. There are others who have recognised that 'development is about power' and feminist and post-colonial scholars have put forward a critique of development studies which this paper builds upon. To intensify their claims, Bandyopadhyay and Patil are happy to include rhetorical questions, ones cited from another paper; 'Is raising race too "distracting, disruptive and demanding"?' 'Does the silence of "race" conceal the complicity of development with racialized projects?' These work as an appeal to the reader to take the issues seriously and perhaps to unsettle reader complacency in a way that other researchers avoid. The value of a counter cultural voice is then that it can disturb a consensus. Researchers take the view that a full-on clash of perspectives is needed rather than a partial critique. An obvious drawback of this more strident approach is that it can turn away those not naturally attracted to a counter cultural position in the first place.

What about your voice?

I have selected articles from journals to illustrate different research voices as these may help you think about which direction you want to go. If you are writing a dissertation or thesis then it is going to take time before you settle into not only understanding the kind of researcher you want to be, but the way in which you want to write. The key then is to recognise there are options in writing a report and to spend time reflecting on these options. It is important, too, to remember that you are not defined as a writer by who you are in everyday life. For example, there are writers who are strident on the page and cautious and modest away from it, and vice versa. The voice is your writer voice, it is a version of yourself that you want to present to your community. You cannot, however, sit down and choose who you are on the page in one go, your voice will develop with experience.

▶ BEING CRITICAL

Being critical is about weighing up the strengths and weaknesses and in presenting your contribution. There is a fine line when it comes to presenting a critical voice between over-confidence, even hubris, 'everything went well and we really need to rethink how we approach this field in the future because of me,' and apologising, 'this was a small project from which it is very difficult to draw generalizable conclusions.' There are 'ifs and buts' in all research but there is always a strength or a contribution on which to comment and often value in drawing attention to *limitations*, rather than weaknesses. The example below presents a methodological strength but also a limitation:

> *A strength of this study was the number of different stakeholders I managed to interview and the engagement of interviewees in the process. However, this was not the case when it came to organisational leaders. I had to negotiate access through secretaries and personal assistants and the interviews themselves were hampered by time constraints. I felt pressured. If I used too much time establishing rapport, I would not be able to complete the interview schedule, but if I focused only getting through the schedule the interview would end up no more than a face-to-face questionnaire. In the event I varied my approach from interviewee to interviewee and did succeed in getting some reflective narratives around leadership. If repeating the study, I would have fewer qualms about going over my allotted time, if allowed to, and I would prioritise rapport over coverage.*

This works well in that a limitation is acknowledged but rather than dwell on it, the student is explaining how it came about and what they did to try to address it. Rather than undermine the reporting, the net result is that the trust between reader and author is strengthened.

Writing demands that you are curious about words, and learning to write critically involves noticing why you are using one word and not another. Even very small changes matter. For example, academics are not agreed as to whether it is *data are* or *data is*. Who cares? I think we should. I prefer data as plural as it helps me think of discrete items rather than an undifferentiated mass, but I realise that it sounds unnatural to some. So, use *data is* if you prefer but know why you are doing it. The little things help you develop a critically aware voice.

Finally, be critical in evaluating the voices of other academics. An easy game to play is to mock the obscure writing of others, but play it carefully. As an example, writing in the 1960s Marcuse wrote a book that has had staying power when it comes to discussion of technology and society. It is often taken as an example of writing that is difficult for the reader to decode. Here, Marcuse (1962:175) discusses linguistic philosophy:

> *Paying respect to the prevailing variety of meanings and usages, to the power and common sense of ordinary speech, while blocking (as extraneous material) analysis of what this speech says about the society that speaks it, linguistic philosophy suppresses once more what is continually suppressed in this universe of discourse and behaviour. The authority of philosophy gives its blessing to the forces which make this universe. Linguistic analysis abstracts from what ordinary language reveals in speaking as it does-the mutilation of man and nature.*

Here, I think Marcuse is expressing a fairly simple idea to the effect that if we only analyse the way that language is constructed, we miss the point that language has the power to rule in or rule out certain ways of thinking. However, it is expressed in a grammatically complex way which is difficult to follow. Marcuse comes over, too, as over-rhetorical, writing of *suppression* and *mutilation* when he is at heart criticising other academics for going about their work in a way he does not like.

Yet, I do not want to go overboard with my critique either. Perhaps the passage suffers as it is taken out of context and would make more sense seen within the entire chapter. Then, Marcuse uses terms in unfamiliar ways (*usages, universe of discourse, authority*) and this is necessarily going to reduce accessibility. Indeed, sometimes lack of clarity can be interesting as it prompts alternative readings of the text. We need to consider too, that Marcuse comes from a tradition of German philosophy and there are expectations around the use of subordinate clauses and sentence constructions that seem odd but are more normal in that tradition. There is then a fine line between criticising and critiquing. There are more than enough academic papers for you to pull apart, but be forgiving if you can.

▶ SUMMARY

This chapter has looked at

- what is common and what is different when it comes to ways of organising a dissertation or thesis
- the importance of editing at whole text, word and sentence level so that you convey your ideas using clear and consistent language
- some of the voices that academics use to convey their ideas in writing
- the importance of editing and proof reading and the time needed to do these tasks properly

The implications for you are to

- identify formats and structures that suit your particular project and be prepared to defend these choices
- appreciate just how long editing and proof reading take and the value of getting feedback on your text
- be clear as to the stance you want to take on social research and present this stance consistently
- be curious about key terms and notice subtleties in meaning
- criticise, but criticise with kindness, the writing of others

▶ WHERE TO READ MORE

There are many guides to writing a thesis or dissertation based on the standard format or variations within such a format. Bell and Waters (2018) is aimed at a general audience, Paltridge and Starfield (2019) at students with ESL and Roush (2018) is aimed at nurse practitioners. There are also a large number of books and articles on practitioner research in general, try McNiff (2017) as a straightforward introduction to action research, and the writing of a practice-based report. Meanwhile Peoples (2020) looks at phenomenology, a distinctive interpretivist approach, in a book that might appeal to a wider audience as it raises general issues around the integration of conceptual and theoretical frameworks in a project report.

There are several books on ethnography which illustrate some of the wider issues at stake in writing for academic audiences. Gullion (2016) is a short accessible guide to writing ethnography while Lewis and Throne (2021) is a much longer exploration of autoethnography and practice-based writing. To reflect on narrative writing you might want to go back to Lewis (2011), first published in 1961, which presents a classic account of a Mexican family. Issues around researchers from the global north researching the global south have been explored critically by recent scholars, including Smith (2021).

There is a quite a literature on students' perspectives of carrying out a research project. Ylijoki (2001) identifies heroic, tragic, business-like, and penal stories of doing research while Kiley (2015) explores different assumptions about theorising held by students from practice and academic backgrounds. Hjortshoj (2018) has a broader reach and looks at blockages on writing and support for the journey from 'student to scholar.'

If you want a radical take on writing social research then try Mol (2003) whose book offers two parallel narratives, the first around her observation of a hospital ward in which atherosclerosis is treated and the second her exploration of related literature. This arrangement serves an ontological purpose as it helps to question the relationship of literature to empirical findings: Do we force concepts on to our data?

I have only briefly covered guides to formatting as every institution will provide guidance of their own. If you do not have enough detail then try to work to the guidelines offered to prospective authors of a journal. These will cover referencing, use of upper case and lower case within the text, formatting, including line spacing and presentation of quotes, and presentation of numbers within a text. Many journals offer good advice on writing for international audiences. If the use of the first person matters to you then go back to Tang and John (1999) in which 'six different identities' behind the use of 'I' in academic writing are identified. A text often cited in support of a straightforward style of writing is Orwell (1946) – it is easily accessed via the Internet.

When it comes to software then most institutions offer guides and run courses on word processing and specialist research software. If not, there are many online guides and just-in-time help in the form of videos on You Tube, or other social networks. Most students avoid attending courses on word processing, after all they can put words on screen and pick up features as they go along. However, if you do not use styles, or captions, and you do not know about automatic tables of contents, then please learn. It will save you time in the long run.

▶ REFERENCES

Bandyopadhyay, R., & Patil, V. (2017). 'The white woman's burden' – The racialized, gendered politics of volunteer tourism. Tourism Geographies, 19(4), 644–657.

Bell, J., & Waters, S. (2018). Doing your research project. Buckingham, UK: Open University Press.

Davis, D. (2021). Presenting research reflexivity in your PhD thesis. Nurse Researcher, 29(1), 37–43.

Geertz, C. (1972). Deep play: Notes on the Balinese cockfight. Daedalus, 101(1), 1–37.

Gullion, J. S. (2016). Writing ethnography. Leiden: Brill.

Hjortshoj, K. (2018). From student to scholar: A guide to writing through the dissertation stage. London: Routledge.

Kiley, M. (2015). 'I didn't have a clue what they were talking about': PhD candidates and theory. Innovations in Education and Teaching International, 52(1), 52–63.

Lewis, C., & Throne, R. (2021). Autoethnography and other self-inquiry methods for practice-based doctoral research. In R. Throne (Ed.), Practice-based and practice-led research for dissertation development (pp. 87–107). Pennsylvania: IGI Global.

Lewis, O. (2011). The children of Sanchez: Autobiography of a Mexican family. New York: Vintage.

López-Martínez, O., & Cuanalo de la Cerda, H.E. (2020). Participatory action research in the design, construction and evaluation of improved cook stoves in a rural Yucatec maya community. Action Research, 18(4), 490–509.

Marcuse, H. (1962). One-dimensional man: Studies in the ideology of advanced industrial society. MA: Beacon Press.

McMillan, D., & Chavis, D. (1986). Sense of community: A definition and theory. Journal of Community Psychology, 14(1), 6–23.

McNiff, J. (2017). Action research: All you need to know. California: SAGE.

Mol, A. (2003). The body multiple. North Carolina: Duke University Press.

Orwell, G. (1946). Politics and the English language. Horizon, April 1946.

Paltridge, B., & Starfield, S. (2019). Thesis and dissertation writing in a second language: A handbook for students and their supervisors. London: Routledge.

Peoples, K. (2020). How to write a phenomenological dissertation: A step-by-step guide. California: SAGE.

Roush, K. (2018). A nurse's step by-step guide to writing a dissertation or scholarly project. Berkshire: Sigma.

Scott-Arthur, T., Brown, B., & Saukko, P. (2021). Conflicting experiences of health and habitus in a poor urban neighbourhood: A Bourdieusian ethnography. Sociology of Health & Illness, 43(3), 697–712.

Segovia-Pérez, M., Castro Núñez, R.B., Santero Sánchez, R., & Laguna Sánchez, P. (2020). Being a woman in an ICT job: An analysis of the gender pay gap and discrimination in Spain. New technology. Work and Employment, 35(1), 20–39.

Smith, L.T. (2021). Decolonizing methodologies: Research and indigenous peoples. London: Zed Books.

Tang, R., & John, S. (1999). The 'I' in identity: Exploring writer identity in student academic writing through the first person pronoun. English for Specific Purposes, 18, S23–S39.

Ylijoki, O. H. (2001). Master's thesis writing from a narrative approach. Studies in Higher Education, 26(1), 21–34.

Final thoughts

In this final chapter we set out:

- A recap of the book
- A holistic approach to academic writing
- Tips for success

▶ A RECAP OF THE BOOK

This book has taken you, the reader, through the process of writing a thesis or dissertation, starting from an initial intention to share experiences with your research community up until the final revising and proof reading of your final report. We have covered this process in five chapters.

Chapter 1 explored the nature of writing, the challenges associated with composing, and the strategies that some people use for overcoming blocks in writing. We took an extended look at planning, drafting, revising, editing, proof reading, and publishing a text on community of practice. Planning was about identifying relevant sources, keeping notes on what you have read and weighing up one text against another. We saw the importance of

DOI: 10.4324/9781003161820-6

frames or structures for writing even if these frames may need to be amended as your writing takes off. Drafting was explained as getting what you want to say put down on the page or screen without worrying too much about the way your text is set out. Use drafting to think through the story and be prepared to see new things as you go along. Revising, editing, and proof reading shifted focus away from content (or composing ideas) to form (transcription into text). We also looked at procrastination when it came to writing and strategies such as episodes of free writing for addressing blockages.

In this first chapter, we also highlighted the importance of understanding audience expectations in regard to the structure and organisation of your text. Here we introduced the idea that the reader, and for you the most important reader of your text is your examiner, wants to see that you can: Show knowledge of your field, discuss methodology and methods, and make a contribution to knowledge. We looked at how you can address these three things in Chapters 2–4.

In Chapter 2, we looked at the place of academic literature, recognising that there were other, very valuable, kinds of knowing, including professional know-how, and personal experience. We described bottom-up and top-down strategies for identifying literature and the pros and cons of each. Reading is taxing and the SQ3R approach to reading was discussed. We then stressed the importance of note taking before going on to look at summarising and paraphrasing. If your notes are clearly organised, the review will take care of itself. Finally, we discussed the special challenges of integrating literature reviews written by others; your role here is to revisit what has been said and to bring in more recent sources.

In Chapter 3, we looked at writing about methods and methodology, starting with a brief discussion of ontology and epistemology – the assumptions we make about the nature of knowledge and how we acquire it. We compared positivism with interpretivism and how your epistemological stance will inform the questions you ask and the assumptions you make about objectivity and causality. We encouraged you to think creatively about epistemology. Many social researchers do not fall into interpretivist and positivist camps and, if this applies to you, be clear when you are shifting from an 'objective' account of a phenomenon to an interpretation of one. It is easy to get drawn into a put down of epistemological positions with which you do not agree; try not to become side-tracked in this way. We looked, too, at how to report data clearly, avoiding excessive use of quotes from participants and unnecessary repetition of what was already clear from tables. Writing about mixed methods creates a challenge as here you need to decide whether data will be reported sequentially or in an integrated fashion. Like so much in social research there is no right or wrong approach.

You were encouraged to be critical. This involved reflecting on the methods and methodology you followed and considering issues of validity, reliability, and trustworthiness. Being critical involved questions of positionality – what are the experiences that led you to interpret the data in a particular way? It was important to keep a positive but balanced stance throughout. There were strengths to any project but limitations in how much data you could collect and the extent to which you can engage with a research context. The decisions taken during the data analysis phase need to be justified.

In Chapter 4, we moved on to making a contribution. We described the importance of addressing the research questions explicitly and comparing your findings to the literature. Consistency with the literature can lend greater credibility to your study but inconsistency should not be dismissed, or wished away. There might be something about the time of your study, the context, or the methodology to explain inconsistency and support your claim to have shed new light on a familiar problem. Indeed, your study may have been triggered by noticing a gap in the literature in the first place.

Readers, and again examiners in particular, want to know how your study helps them understand the problem or field you are researching. This may mean introducing new ideas ('here is a concept which will help others discuss a problem in a different way') and/or new models ('here factors are identified and relationships between the factors are explained'). We stressed that moving from description to explanation and on to theorising was a challenge but one that you were expected to take on when writing a dissertation or thesis. It was important, finally, that you set out recommendations for different stakeholders, recognising that you can only advise not tell people what they should do.

We turned in Chapter 5 to the presentation of the thesis and how to put it all together. We briefly described the way that titles, abstracts, and introductions worked together to set out the big idea of your study. In most institutions we saw that there was a lot of focus on the standard format for writing a thesis or dissertation. This was understandable as this format was easy for the reader to follow, offering as it does a step-by-step approach. However, there were other formats that might better cater for narrative, practice, and grounded theory reporting.

We then moved to the organisation of a report at chapter, section, and sentence level. Where possible try to avoid overlong chapters, sections, and sentences. In general, academic writing tries to be concise and accessible for the reader but there was no getting away from the fact that social research is dealing with complex ideas. There is a specialised vocabulary associated with academic research and entering an academic community involves understanding the nuances of particular terms and the exact meanings they convey.

We went on to show that there were many different voices in academia but like the standard format there was a standard voice: Objective, as far as that was possible, modest, formal, and cautious. However, variations were possible. Some academics had more reflective, narrative, or practitioner voices and some presented a more strident counter cultural voice intended to unsettle a consensus. You can be influenced by others but you need to find your own way of writing.

▶ A HOLISTIC APPROACH TO ACADEMIC WRITING

The book has set out with three different kinds of knowledge that you need to call on when writing a thesis or dissertation. First, knowledge of writing itself and an appreciation of the goal of contributing to a research community; second, knowledge of research practices including reporting of literature, showing understanding of epistemology, applying methods, reporting and discussing findings; third, an understanding of academic writing, how it is structured and the different voices within it.

My argument is that you need to call on all three types of knowledge and see writing a dissertation or thesis as a joined up or holistic practice (see Figure 6.1). It is not enough to know about the nature of writing or the form that academic writing should take if you do not know how to discuss research methods or weigh up evidence for the claims you are making. It is not enough to know about theories in your particular field if you cannot write about how they informed your work in a clear and concise way. And it is not enough to know all there is to know about interview as a method if you cannot organise a coherent account of what you did and why you did it.

Joining up these three different kinds of knowledge is not easy. However, there are some strategies to help. Recognise when you are procrastinating and step away from writing when you need to give yourself time. Try to get into productive habits of writing. Use diagrams and tables as frames or structures and find models that help you in organising your text. Writing is a private activity, it is you left alone with your thoughts, but you can engage with your peers and your supervisor through sharing work in progress and do ask for feedback from anyone willing to give it. Read what others have written – are there structures to follow? As you write do not lose track of your goals in undertaking the research: What exactly did you set out to address, what were the gaps and how should different stakeholders see the problem now you have carried out this study?

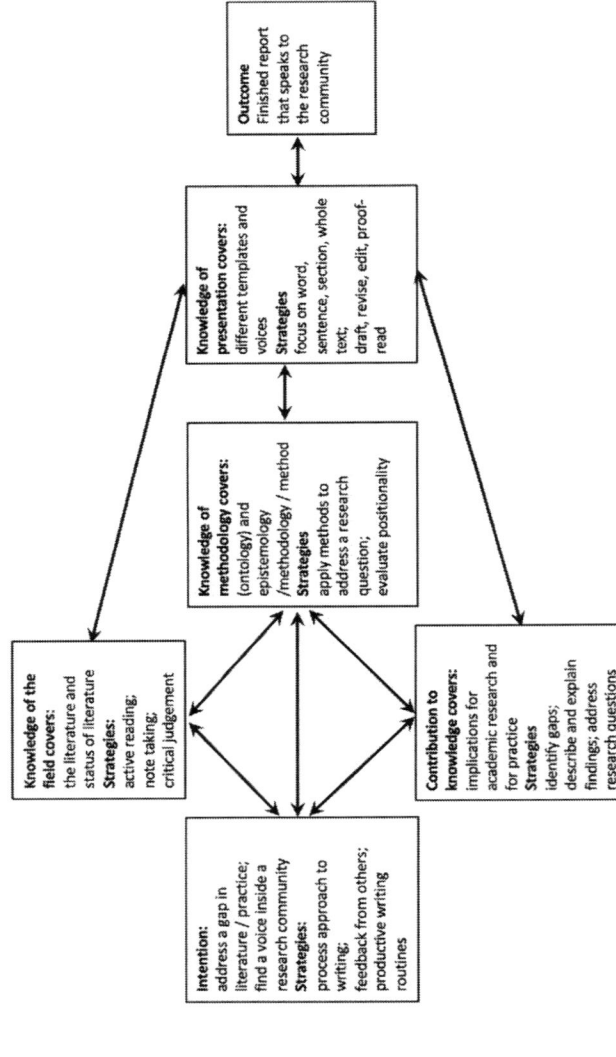

Figure 6.1 A joined-up approach to writing a thesis or dissertation

▶ TIPS FOR SUCCESS

A successful dissertation or thesis is one that you are proud of and look back on with fondness. You, the writer, are an excellent judge of what you set out to do and how much you achieved. But it is not all about you. A piece of writing also needs to be judged by the reader. Readers, as you know yourself as you are a reader, are often exacting and want to know they can trust you. You do not need to pander to your readers' prejudices to get them onside, rather you need to convince them you have something to say that is worth saying. You are telling them, 'I want to take you on a journey, I promise it will be worthwhile so spend some time in my company'. Make it easy for readers to follow what you did, do not leave them guessing as to the significance of what you have found out. This book gives you the big picture of the different kinds of knowledge and skills on which you need to draw in order to be a persuasive academic writer. Before finishing though I would like to offer some smaller take-aways for your next episode of academic writing.

1 *Work at your own pace:* Break down the available time into doable writing targets for each day. Find a routine that gives you time to think and even to daydream. Be easy on yourself. Writing really is a challenge and it takes time, feedback, and self-discipline.
2 *When you get stuck in writing it is for a reason:* Use strategies such as free writing to move on. Sometimes you are not ready to write and you need to take time out to read more or to talk to others – or to yourself.
3 *Do not slavishly follow any specific advice anyone gives you about writing a dissertation or thesis but pay attention to the spirit in which it is offered:* You really do not need to read following a SQ3R model but you do need to find a way to avoid passive reading. There is no need to break down writing into five steps, but you do need to think how to manage the shift from composing to transcribing. You do not have to learn thirty different ways of connecting two sentences together but you do have to choose vocabulary carefully.

4 *Templates are really useful for writing but should not suffocate you*: Whichever template you are using, aks yourself whether it reflects the way you want to write about your project.

5 *Make the research question(s) that runs through your thesis or dissertation explicit*: Show the reader how you began by identifying a problem and why this problem was worth investigating. Describe how you addressed the research question(s) and explain how the problem should be seen differently now you have carried out the research. Use signposts and summaries to guide the reader.

6 *Do not understate your contribution to knowledge*: When writing about your research be assertive, make claims and provide the evidence to support them. Remember you are researching at a particular time and in a particular place which no-one has done before. You have read intensively about your topic and, best of all, you are seeing the problem with fresh eyes. You have something to say that is worth saying.

7 *Do not overstate your contribution to knowledge:* Be assertive but also reflective. Show that alternative approaches were possible and there were limitations in your study. Accept that there is more to read and more to know. Being open about your limitations may strengthen rather than weaken your argument.

8 *Provide both the small and the big picture:* Discuss methodologies and methods in general but bring this discussion back to what you did in your particular project and the opportunities and difficulties you experienced. Discuss wider debates in your field but identify the practical implications for your project too.

9 *Be wary of rigid binary distinctions:* Methods can be broken down between interpretivist v positivist; quantitative v qualitative; top-down v bottom-up. But while these distinctions can be helpful most social research deals with mixed epistemologies and varied strategies.

10 *You do not need to have a special talent for writing to write a valuable research report:* Simply draft and redraft until you are expressing yourself clearly. Revise and edit so that you are concise and using a consistent structure and vocabulary. Do not forget to state the obvious.

11 *Editing and proofreading really matters*: This is not about following old fashioned rules about splitting infinitives or starting a sentence with *and* or *but*. It is about respecting the reader by ensuring there are as few typos and clumsy expressions as possible.

12 *Learn to see your text through the eyes of the reader and the community you are writing for*: Your goal is to add your voice to the academic community. To do this you need to show you understand your community's concerns and ways of working even if you want to critique some of what goes on.

Finally, can I encourage you to keep writing? After finishing a thesis or dissertation, you may be looking forward to undertaking more research and perhaps you are considering an academic career. Alternatively, you might decide you never want to do academic research again. But whatever you, do not stop writing. If academic writing is not your thing, then do not give up on writing for professional audiences, or writing blogs for whoever wants to read them, or writing notes for yourself. Write poems and drama if you do not want to write prose. Take advantage of any opportunities you have to make your voice heard, not just by the people you meet in person but by communities removed from you in time and distance. We all need to know what you have to say.

Key terms

Bibliography: A list of all of the sources you have used (whether you have referenced them or not) in the process of carrying out your project. For reasons of space, most reports now only list references, i.e. sources cited in the report.

Citation: The source that you have drawn on. The cited author(s) can be the subject of the sentence: 'A (2010) argues that reading is an important aspect of study' or 'A (2010) argued that reading was an important aspect of study'. Alternatively, authors could be cited in support of a position, for example, 'reading is an important aspect of academic study (see A, 2000; B, 2020; C, 2009)'.

Clarity: Here the use of signposting and sequencing to lead the reader through the text, and the attention to detail when introducing vocabulary and key terms. Clarity is to some extent in the eye of the reader. A text could be clearly set out, but still inaccessible if the reader lacks the background knowledge to find meaning in it.

Cohesion: Closely aligned to clarity. The way that a text hangs together. Linguists are particularly interested in how the writer refers back to previous parts of a text and their use of connecting words and phrases to join up ideas.

Common knowledge: What is held in common between speakers or, in our case, between authors and reader. Thus, the reader need not repeat in-depth arguments with which the reader is familiar as this is common knowledge.

Composing: Here, the drafting of the text, i.e. getting words on the page.

Concise: Putting an idea across using as few words as needed.

Contraction: Shortened forms such as *isn't, can't, won't*. For historical reasons, these are avoided in academic articles.

Criticality: Weighing up a stance or point of view as objectively as possible and using evidence to support one's argument.

Density: Percentage of a message that is focused on content in contrast to function (e.g. the use auxiliary verbs and conversation fillers). Thus, written text is often denser than speech.

Draft: A work in progress version of a text.

Editing: A run through of the text checking on use of appropriate vocabulary, grammar, and sentence construction.

Epistemology: A stance on how knowledge is acquired, for example, interpretivism and positivism are epistemological positions.

Ethnography: Here, the researcher tries to enter the social world of the people being studied. This usually involves a long-term immersion in a family, school, hospital, playground, office, etc.

Experimental method: The investigation, in a controlled context, of the impact of one variable on another as measured by observable outcomes. It involves comparison between an experimental group, members of which receive an intervention, and control group, whose members do not.

Formal and informal language: Formality is conveyed through sentence length, grammar, for example, use of contractions or not, and choice of vocabulary. 'The person with whom he is talking' is formal and 'the person he's chatting to' is informal. It is often thought that formal words are longer and have origins and in Latin and Greek (e.g. conversing, discoursing, deliberating), while informal words (yabbering, chattering) have their origins in Anglo-Saxon.

Genre: Socially agreed-upon conventions that make it possible to categorise different types of texts and outputs. Academic writing as a genre is shown by formal organisation of chapters and sections, the use signalling and sequencing, and the use of citations as evidence. Typically, academic writing uses more formal vocabulary. Within this one genre there are sub-genres, for example, narrative ethnography, reflective practice writing.

Hedging: Expressing caution in your claims by, for example, the use of modal verbs ('the results *might* suggest') or adverbs of frequency ('a reason for this was *probably...*').

Impact factor: A calculation based on number of times articles in a journal have been cite. This is used as a rough measure of the standing of the journal within a field.

Literature review: A summary of what has been written about a topic, and the main approaches to researching it.

Meta-analysis: A particular type of literature review which aggregates the findings from quantitative studies.

Method: The means through which data are gathered within a research study. Methods include interviewing, questionnaire survey, and observation.

Methodology: The rationale that the researcher offers for the application of particular research methods. Methodology could include action research, case study, ethnography, experimental methods, and case study.

Ontology: A stance on the nature of being and existence. In social research, this often concerns beliefs about the nature of reality, in particular social reality. On one hand, some believe an objective reality exists independent of the observer, but others believe reality is always perceived subjectively.

Paraphrasing: To express the main idea from another's work in one's own words.

Patchworking: Taking chunks of text from different sources and merging them in a text with no attempt to acknowledge the original sources.

Peer review: The review of one's work by fellow academics before acceptance, or rejection, in an academic journal.

Plagiarism: Passing off someone else's ideas as your own.

Proof reading: The reading of a text in order to correct typographical and other transcription errors.

Qualifying: Expressing caution or uncertainty in what you are claiming. Qualifying is similar to hedging but is more associated with bringing in other sources of evidence or showing there are other ways of looking at the data, rather than with language forms.

Redundancy: An unnecessary repetition of information often resulting in tautology, for example, 'redundancy involves repetition of ideas and phrases making such repetition redundant.'

Revising: Making changes to the structure of the text once a first draft has been completed.

Scanning: Reading so as to pick out a specific idea or item in the text.

Skimming: Reading so as to quicky get the general idea of a text.

SQ3R: A strategy for reading based on *Survey, Question, Read, Recall*, and *Review*.

Summarising: Presenting the key ideas from a text in a more concise form. Generally involves expressing the original idea in one's own words even if using some of the key terms from the original.

Systematic review: A summary of the literature that uses 'objective' criteria to identify articles to include and explicit procedures for analysis.

Text: In media studies text covers written material (e.g. articles, books), visual material (e.g. films, works of art), aural material (e.g. songs, interview), and multimedia material (e.g. web sites). Texts are written for removed audiences, i.e. a spoken lecture is not a text but a recording of the lecture posted on the internet is.

Transcribing: Putting something into a written form as in transcribing an interview. Transcriptions can be verbatim, i.e. they contain all that was said including fillers such as um and er, and signal laughter or crying.

Transferability: The application of findings from one inquiry to another context.

Transition: Moving from one topic or one idea to another.

Unit of meaning: A part of a text that carries a function or meaning for a reader, it could be a phrase, sentence, or something larger.

Writing frame: Something which sets out the expected structure of a text, for example, a mind map, section titles, and/or first sentences for each paragraph.

Index

Printed in Dunstable, United Kingdom